A GREAT WEEKEND IN

# VENICE

# A GREAT WEEKEND IN
# VENICE

Venice, (the Serenissima) a city famous for its waterways, has been charming people since the Middle Ages, and has no intention of changing. Like the endless succession of writers, painters, musicians and film-makers who have come here before you, and the many thousands of visitors who are stunned by Venice's beauty each year, you too will undoubtedly fall under its magical spell.

As you explore Venice, the palaces of the Grand Canal, St Mark's Square with its pigeons, and the gondolas gliding silently across the lagoon all help bring this magical city to life. The churches and museums, the festivals that have been celebrated for decades, the sumptuous cafés with their sunlit terraces, the famous jewellers and the luxury fabric and antique shops will all enchant you.

And when you wander along its winding alleyways, Venice will reveal itself to be so much more than just a museum city or tempting shopping centre. It will surprise you by revealing its other face, that of a city with secret and charming residential districts. As you stroll through the city, you may find yourself walking alongside a quiet *rio,* where market-gardeners' boats overflowing with fruit and vegetables are moored, before emerging into a little *campo* full of children playing. Next minute, you may have to elbow your way through a narrow *calle*. Carried along by the crowd, you may sometimes find it difficult to stop to look in the tempting shop windows full of Murano glass or Burano lace, the *legatorie* (stationery shops) with their unique marbled paper, the grocer's shops with their rainbow-coloured pasta,

or the mask shops where skilled craftsmen work with leather or papier mâché.

In the evening, after a memorable dinner at a little *osteria*, you'll find plenty of other pleasures in store for you. You may decide to go to a theatre, where you'll be enchanted by the works of Goldoni; to listen to the music of Vivaldi beneath the vaults of a Gothic church; to drift in a gondola on the illuminated Grand Canal or to have a drink in one of the city's many bars – it's up to you. All you have to do is choose between the city's many attractions. But be warned – it won't be easy!

However you decide to spend your time, the weekend will simply fly by. And once you've fallen under its spell, Venice will draw you back time and again.

# How to get to there

## WHEN TO GO

### THE BEST TIME OF YEAR

In winter, the Adriatic coast is often cold and windswept. In addition to the Bora, freezing cold air accompanied by a few snowflakes sometimes blows down from the neighbouring Alps. If you time your visit to coincide with the Carnival, remember to take some warm clothes, including coats, gloves and raincoats. It can rain in Venice until the end of spring and an *acqua alta* can happen at any time in winter. The waters of the lagoon rise and flood the city centre, making it impossible to get about.

The best time of year is from late April to early July, when visitors first begin to arrive in droves. In late spring, it rains less often, the air is mild and the long days allow you to dine out of doors in the light of the setting sun.

Summer isn't necessarily the best time of

year to visit Venice. Apart from the crowds of tourists, the air can be unpleasantly humid. Clouds of insects, including mosquitoes (*zanzare*), sometimes take advantage of the climate to invade the lagoon and the water can be smelly.

The autumn, from September to November, is the other good time of

year to visit Venice. The days are shorter but the light is beautiful.

The islands of the lagoon are sometimes noisy with migrating birds stopping off on their way to warmer climes. The weather is still fine and though there can be showers, they often don't last long. However, the nights are cool from September onwards.

Your choice of season may, of course, depend on the large number of festivals and other events taking place in the city. See page 21 for exact dates.

## HOW TO GET THERE

### FROM THE UK

**Go** (☎ 0845 6054321 www.go-fly.com) and **British Airways** (☎ 0345 222111) fly direct to Venice. Ryan Air

### THE ORIENT EXPRESS

This luxury train takes you from London or Paris to Venice in around 30 hours from London and 24 from Paris.
You travel through magical landscapes (via Innsbruck, the Brenner Pass, the Dolomites and Verona) aboard luxurious 1930s-style carriages, enjoying delicious cuisine all the way.
The return journey is by plane and the trip costs from around £1500, with 2 nights in Venice.

(☎ 0541 569569) flies to Treviso Airport, which is a short train or bus ride from Venice.

### FROM IRELAND

There are no direct flights from Ireland to vVenice. Most flights, including with Ryan Air and British Airways are via London.

### FROM ELSEWHERE

There are no direct flights from the United States, Canada, Australia or New Zealand. However, the following major airlines can arrange your connection to Venice with a code share or another airline from major European hubs, usually London or Rome.

**Alitalia**
www.alitalia.com
Their website is packed with flight information and includes contact details for their offices worldwide.

**Air Canada**
www.aircanada.ca
Flies to Rome via Frankfurt or London.

**American Airlines**
www.americanairlines.com
Flies to Rome via London, Brussels or Zurich.

**Cathay Pacific**
www.cathaypacific.com
Fly daily from Sydney and Melbourne via Hong Kong.

## VENICE AND ITALY ONLINE

**www.venetia.it** is a comprehensive Venice guide including maps, calendar of events and cultural information and history.

**www.itg.com** claims to have everything you need to know to plan your trip to Italy.

**www.italytour.com** includes tourist and cultural information for Italy.

**www.initaly.com** has information on travel and accommodation in Italy.

### Qantas
www.qantas.com
Fly twice a week direct from Sydney to Rome.

### Singapore Airlines
www.singaporeair.com
They operate a daily service from Australia and New Zealand to Singapore. From there they have connecting flights to Italy three days per week.

## ARRIVING AT THE AIRPORT

Marco Polo Airport is on the mainland north-east of the city. There are ticket machines in the departures hall and the bureau de change is open 24 hours a day.

The most pleasant way to reach the city centre is by waterbus, landing near Piazza S. Marco, with stops at Murano and the Lido. There are departures every hour on average from 6am to midnight. The journey takes 50 minutes and costs L17,000 You buy your ticket before boarding on the left of the exit in the arrivals hall. Watertaxis do the same dream crossing (minus the detour to the Lido) in only 20 minutes, but for six times the price (allow around L150,000 to get to the city centre). Lastly, you have the option of the blue bus, which goes direct for L5,000, or taxis, which take you to Piazzale Roma in 15-20 minutes for L25,000.

## INCLUSIVE BREAKS

Many tour operators offer two and three-day weekend breaks that include travel (by plane, train or coach) and accommodation in various categories of hotel. For the best rates, you have to spend Saturday night in Venice.

The main advantage of these breaks is that they give you the chance to stay at a luxury hotel for a very reasonable price. You also benefit from the rates negotiated by tour operators and travel more cheaply while avoiding the bother of booking.

## BUDGETING FOR THE TRIP

It has to be said that Venice is an expensive city, even though the lire is relatively under-valued.

Transport costs around 30 % more than in France, a museum ticket costs F35-45, a coffee costs from F5 (standing at the counter) to F40 (at the Florian, the best café in Venice).

A restaurant meal costs F100-350 per person according to category, but the thing that will add most to the cost of your trip is undoubtedly your hotel room (around F800 a night in a 3-star hotel.

## AVERAGE TEMPERATURES IN °C/°F

|            | MINIMUM      | MAXIMUM      |
|------------|--------------|--------------|
| JAN.-MAR.  | 1-5/34-41    | 6-12/43-54   |
| APR.-JUN.  | 10-18/50-64  | 17-25/63-77  |
| JUL.-SEP.  | 20-17/68-63  | 28-25/82-77  |
| OCT.-DEC.  | 11-2/52-36   | 12-8/54-46   |

## CURRENCY

Italy is one of the European Union countries that joined the single currency, and from 2002 the Euro will replace the Lira. 1 Euro = L1936.27. In the meantime, all prices are listed in both Lire and Euros. Bureaux de change charge 2·8% commission, so changing cash or traveller's cheques once you get there is relatively expensive.

It's more economical to take Eurocheques or make full use of your credit card, especially to settle your restaurant and hotel bills, and to pay for things you buy in shops. You can get cash for incidental expenses from cash machines at advantageous rates for a flat-rate commission of just F15.

Bear in mind that it's impossible to withdraw less than L100,000 (around £30) from cash machines in Italian banks.

## WHAT TO PACK

In spring and summer, take light clothes, a jumper for the evenings, which can be cool, and for boat trips to the islands, as well as a swimsuit if you want to take a dip in the sea from the Lido beach. In late autumn and winter, remember to take warm

## CHECK THE PRICES

If prices in baker's, grocer's and other food shops seem abnormally low, take a closer look. You're sure to see *etto*, meaning hectogram (100gm/3$^1$/2oz), written on the label.

In Italy in general and Venice in particular, prices are very often given per 100gm/3$^1$/2oz rather than per kilo/2·2lb.

In restaurants, prices are often given by weight, per 100gm/3$^1$/2oz. Your portion of meat or fish will therefore be weighed before it's brought to the table.

Finally, make sure you always check the bill.

too, though it may be hard to handle in the narrow streets. And, whatever the season, take something smart to wear when you go to the theatre or out to dinner, as well as a good pair of shoes. Treading the *calle* and walking up and down over the bridges may not seem like much, but it actually puts tender feet to the test. Mosquito-repellent cream is also very useful for keeping the dreaded insects at bay. With all the stagnant water about, there are swarms of them in summer.

## FORMALITIES

Citizens of the European Union must have a valid identity card or passport. Travellers from the USA, Canada, Australia and New Zealand require a valid passport and are limited to a 90-day stay.

clothes and windproofs (to protect you from the biting east wind in particular). An umbrella can be very useful,

## HEALTH

No vaccinations are necessary before entering the country. If you fall ill, you may have to pay for your treatment, but you can be reimbursed. Before departure, get an E111 form from the post office to claim a refund of any medical expenses incurred.

## LOCAL TIME

Italy is one hour ahead of Greenwich Mean Time. Summertime starts at the end of March, when clocks are put forward an hour, and wintertime at the end of September, when clocks go back an hour.

## INSURANCE

UK tour operators are obliged by law to offer insurance covering loss of possessions and health and repatriation insurance but not cancellation and luggage insurance. If you pay for your plane or train ticket with an international credit card, you're automatically entitled to good cover for medical expenses and the cost of repatriation. Otherwise, it's best to take out cover for the cost of repatriation with a well-known, reputable insurance company

### USEFUL ADDRESSES

**Italian State Tourist Board**
1 Princes Street, London W1
☎ 020 7408 1254
📠 020 7493 6695

**Italian Consulate**
38 Eaton Place, London SW1
☎ 020 7235 9371

**Italian Cultural Institute**
39 Belgrave Square
London SW1
☎ 020 7235 1461
📠 020 7235 4618

**Italian Book Shop**
8 Cecil Court, London WC2
☎ 020 7240 1634

**Citalia (Italian tourist agency)**
Marco Polo House
3-5 Lansdowne Rd
Croydon CR9 1LL
☎ 020 8686 5533
📠 020 8681 0712
e-mail ciao@citalia.co.uk

**Italian Government Travel Offices outside the UK**

630 5th Avenue,
New York, NY
☎ 212 245 4822
📠 212 586 9249

550, 12400 Wiltshire Bvd
Los Angeles, Ca
☎ 310 820 1898
📠 310 820 6357

1914, 1 Place Ville-Marie
Montreal, Canada
☎ 514 866 7668
📠 514 866 7667

c/o Italian Chamber of Commerce and Industry
Level 26, 44 Market St, Sydney
☎ 292 621666
📠 292 625745

# VENICE ON SHOW

## FROM THE POMP OF BYZANTIUM TO THE FIREWORKS OF TIEPOLO

Since the Middle Ages, Venice, the Serenissima, has never ceased to fascinate the ambassadors, kings and travellers who have visited it. Every conceivable art form – gilded mosaics, countless pictures, numerous painted ceilings, grandiose sculpture and architecture, and even musicians, have served to enhance the splendour of this very unusual city.

### FROM BYZANTINE GOLD TO GOTHIC ELEGANCE

It was only natural for Venice, a former colony of Constantinople, to turn first to Byzantine art. But it put its own particular stamp on it, expressing a need for its own brand of elegance. In the 11th century, for example, a Romanesque-influenced apse was grafted onto the Basilica San Marco. The same thing happened the following century at S. S. Maria e Donato, which is reflected in the water of the Canal Grande of Murano.

Enriched by trade with the Orient, Venice only adopted the Gothic style in the late 14th century. The architects of the Doges' palace designed the heavy mass of the first floor to be supported by stone tracery, and had no hesitation in reversing the traditional laws of architecture. In palaces and churches elsewhere, builders favoured slender lines and florid decoration.

### VENICE AND THE RENAISSANCE

The Renaissance only came into its own on the lagoon in the 16th century. The architect Sansovino (1470–1529), who designed the loggia of the campanile of the Basilica San Marco, and above all Andrea Palladio (1508–1580), who was responsible for the geometrical forms of the Redentore on the Giudecca and San Giorgio Maggiore, are the two best representatives of the movement. It was at this time that Venetian painting produced its most talented artists. Giovanni Bellini (c.1430–1516),

*The Assumption by Titian (1517).*

## VENICE, THE CRADLE OF OPERA

In 1637, a troupe of strolling players

the inventor of the golden light that resembles the mosaics of San Marco, trained the subtle artist Giorgione (c.1477–1510) and the 'king of painters', Titian (c.1488–1576). Vittore Carpaccio (1455–1526) immortalised the Venetian festivals, while Tintoretto (1518–1594) and Veronese (1528–1588) carried on the theatrical, and specifically Venetian, tradition.

### THE BAROQUE PERIOD AND THE ENLIGHTENMENT

In the 17th century, Venice was the victim of repeated plague epidemics and economic crises. Artistic production suffered as a result, but nevertheless continued until the late 18th century and included

such famous names as the architect Baldassare Longhena (1598–1682), who designed Santa Maria della Salute, and the playwright Carlo Goldoni (1707–1793), who wrote around a hundred comedies. Painting flourished: to the work of landscape artists such as Antonio Canaletto (1697–1768) and Francesco

performed an opera in a public theatre in Venice. The experiment was such a success that theatres sprang up everywhere and an art form developed through which Venice could express its love of stage sets and machinery, in other words its need for show. Every period since has given rise to masterpieces that have exerted a considerable influence on European opera as a whole, including the operas of Monteverdi (1567–1643), Cavalli (1602–1676), Vivaldi (1678–1741) and the master of *bel canto*, Rossini (1792–1868).

Gaudi (1712–1792), who portrayed the Serenissima in all its forms, was added the genre painting of Pietro Longhi (1702–1785) and the marvellous talent of Gianbattista Tepolo (1696–1770). With these artists the Venetian school ended in a grand display of trompe-l'œil and colour.

*San Geremia and the Palazzo Labia, Venice.*

# POMP AND CIRCUMSTANCE

## PALACES STANDING IN WATER

Starting with a number of constraints, such as the absence of streets, the predominance of water and the palaces' dual role as shops and residences, the Venetian architects erected monuments that suited both changing fashions and their heritage. Their common efforts over the centuries have made the Grand Canal the most beautiful street in the world.

### THE FIRST PALACES
(12TH–13TH CENTURY)

The oldest palaces in Venice date from the 13th century and bear the mark of Byzantine influence. Their façades are recognisable by the arcaded portico covering practically the whole of the ground floor (merchandise was unloaded here), as at the Fondaco dei Turchi, on the banks of the Grand Canal. Decoration remained discreet and for defensive reasons there were few openings.

### THE GOTHIC PALACE
(13TH–15TH CENTURY)

Times had changed, and Venice had become an opulent city. The middle classes, who had grown rich on trade, and

the great noble families now wanted more comfortable, better-lit residences. The most sumptuous of them all, the Ca' d'Oro, displays the characteristics that were all the rage at that time. Its façade (which was originally covered in gold) opens onto the Grand Canal by means of intertwined Gothic arches resembling lacy ribbons, and ornate windows that catch the light. Everywhere you look, fine decoration accentuates the slender lines of the palace and adds to its elegance.

Vendramin Calergi (the site of the winter casino) and Palazzo Corner, both of which are on the Grand Canal, were built in brick instead of sandstone. They henceforth presented an imposing façade embellished by the horizontal and vertical lines of cornices and pilasters (antique columns). The windows opened onto balconies and had exchanged their broken arcading for round arches.

## THE STRUCTURE OF THE PALACES AND HOUSES

While the façades of the *palazzi* (the *Ca'*, the diminutive of *casa*, or 'house' in Italian), on which every care was lavished, evolved and followed the dictates of fashion, their internal structure changed little over the centuries. Three floors were more or less the rule up to the 18th century. The ground floor, which was accessible by boat, housed shops and a large central space (the *portego*). The first floor (*piano nobile*) was reserved for offices and, in the grand palaces, sumptuously decorated reception rooms. The patrician families lived on the airier second floor and the servants lived in the attic. Venetian residences were grouped round a courtyard, which provided essential ventilation. The courtyard was square in the Middle Ages, but rectangular in shape from the Renaissance onwards. It was extended on the side by a *rio* or *calle*.

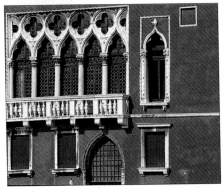

## THE RENAISSANCE PALACE
(15TH–16TH CENTURY)
Monumentality, symmetry and harmony were the keywords of Renaissance architecture. The 16th-century palaces, such as Palazzo

## THE BAROQUE PALACE
(17TH CENTURY)
The Baroque taste for the theatrical triumphed on the Grand Canal with Ca' Pesaro, the palace built by Baldassare Longhena in the mid-17th century. Unlike his Renaissance counterparts, the architect left not a single surface unadorned. Garlands, trophies, monstrous faces and diamond-shaped bosses enlivened the whole of the façade, which attained an unrivalled degree of opulence.

# WRITING *ALLA VENEZIANA*

## VENETIAN MARBLED PAPER AND STATIONERY

Less than fifty years after the discovery of the printing press, Venice had become the European capital of printing, thanks to the efforts of the humanist printer, Alde Manuce (1449–1515), who invented italic letters. Ink, pens and the famous marbled paper, of which the Venetians are so proud, are still made by craftsmen today.

## A SHORT HISTORY OF MARBLED PAPER

The existence of marbled paper is documented in Japan in the 13th century. Later, in the 15th and 16th centuries, the technique spread to Persia and then to Turkey, where it was called *ebrû*, after the floral design still perpetuated by the *legatoria* of Alberto Valese (see p. 89). Around the 18th century, Western bookbinders used marbled paper *en masse* to cover books. Calfskin had become too expensive and was now only used for the spines, while the flyleaves were covered in paper. It became such a craze that craftsmen used it to make a wide variety of objects, including boxes of every possible shape and size – a craft tradition that Venice has preserved intact in its entirety.

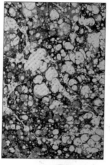

## MARBLED PAPERMAKING

Imagine a drop of oil floating on the surface of water. If a sheet of paper is placed delicately on top of it, the colour is transferred onto the paper, leaving the water clear. This is the basic principle of marbled papermaking. The craftsman throws drops of colour mixed with oxgall into a marbling

with a negative of the colour bath. All he then has to do is leave it to dry before starting all over again from square one.

tank. The drops spread over the surface of the water, which is denser. He then repeats the process with the next colour in order to create veining.

Once this delicate preparation is complete (the more colours there are, the more likely they are to smudge), he creates designs with a brush or gently 'pulls' the colours using a point, then a comb, in order to obtain lines. He next places a sheet of paper on the surface of the water, which becomes impregnated

## THE DIFFERENT TYPES OF MARBLED PAPER

**Pebbled**: the colours are not combed, and the pebbling (involving two or three colours) resembles cell tissue as seen under a microscope.

**Marbled**: as its name suggests, this resembles marble with veining of one or more colours; it's an elegant paper suitable for bookbinding.

**Partridge eye and peacock feather marbling**: two shimmering designs often involving four colours that are reminiscent of the birds of their name; these designs are the most difficult to produce

because of the danger of the colours mingling.

**Ebrû**: the craftsman draws floral designs, and the marbled paper produced is probably the most beautiful of all. It is also the one that depends most on the individual creativity of the craftsman.

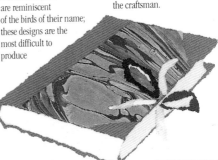

# VENETIAN FABRICS
## SILK AND VELVET OF EVERY KIND

Since the age when Venice was the nerve centre of European trade, it has remained the home of luxury fabrics. The incredibly sumptuous hand-printed damasks, silks and brocades that you'll find here – some of which are hand woven – are sure to dazzle you with their beauty.

## FORTUNY, THE ANDALUSIAN TURNED VENETIAN

Mariano Fortuny Y Madrazo (1871–1949) settled in Venice in 1888, in Palazzo Pesaro degli Orfei. He set up a workshop on the first floor and indulged his passion for the theatre and stage costumes in particular. He designed the Cnossos scarf in 1906, and his first Delphos dress the following year, a clinging taffeta garment reminiscent of the charioteer of Delphi. Fortuny later designed a famous lamp (see box) and a whole range of pleated velvets and silk or cotton garments that emphasised the figure and profoundly influenced fashion at the start of the century.

## FORTUNY PLEATS

The pleats are made by hand in damp fabric, then sewn in place and fixed with a hot iron. To preserve them, the silk is twisted into skeins. Examples of this technique (scarves in particular) can be seen in the window of Venetia Studium (see p. 91), whose creations use Fortuny's technique to the letter.

## THE DESIGNS

Fortuny used écru velvet or cotton, which he brushed with metallic colours to add a base tone. The designs, which took their inspiration from the Orient, and above all from the Venetian Renaissance, were then stencilled on. They were sometimes combined with a fine network of gold or silver thread. All the Fortuny fabric designs produced on the island of the Giudecca can be found at the shop Trois (see p. 91). Other major manufacturers, including Gaggio (see p. 90), also produce hand-printed designs reminiscent of those of Fortuny.

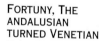

## SILK AND VELVET WEAVING

The silk damasks and sumptuous iridescent velvets of the firm Rubelli (see p. 90) and the house of Bevilacqua (see p. 90) – the two big names in Venetian fabrics – are made on antique looms dating from as far back as the 18th century. To give an idea of the work involved, a worker and her assistant only make a strip 40cm/15¾in long by 60cm/23½in wide in a day (the maximum allowed by a hand loom). This explains the prohibitive price of these fabrics. The other silks and velvets, which are sold in a standard width (130cm/51in), are made on mechanical looms and are therefore far less expensive.

## FORTUNY LAMP

Venetia Studium (see p. 91) is the only place where you can still buy lamps like the ones made by Mariano Fortuny. The silk is placed on the metal frames of the lampshades, then decorated with delicate hand-painted floral designs using gold, silver and other colours. The edge is decorated with Murano blown-glass beads. The lamps take a team of a dozen craftsmen several days to make, which goes a long way to explaining their astronomically high prices.

## MORE AFFORDABLE ACCESSORIES

Most of the fabric manufacturers of Venice sell small objects made of hand-printed silk or velvet. These are the things to go for if you want to bring a little Venetian chic back with you. Women will fall for the small purses by Bevilacqua or the pleated velvet scarves by Venetia Studium, while men will go for the ties at Gaggio (see p. 90).

# ROMANTIC VENICE
## HAND IN HAND IN THE SERENISSIMA

If you were looking for the ideal place to spend a honeymoon, you couldn't do better than Venice. It's won the votes of generations of lovers the world over. But newly-weds aren't the only ones who can enjoy a romantic stroll in the Serenissima. Here are a few tips for anyone who'd like to go for a quiet walk in this most glittering of cities.

*The Hotel Danieli*

means of transport is concerned, you can either go for speed – in which case you'll come by plane, then take a taxi-boat to reach the city – or for elegant surroundings combined with gourmet food, in which case, you'll opt for the Orient Express (see p. 5), a luxury train with an irresistible 1920s flavour.

## GETTING READY FOR THE JOURNEY

Go to your travel agents and book a room in an 18th-century palace or one of the finest luxury hotels in the city, such as the Gritti (see p. 41) or the Danieli (see p. 59). As far as the

## WHERE TO GO AND WHAT TO DO

The best place to start is in the Piazza San Marco. Visit the basilica, climb to the top of the bell tower, buy a

piece of jewellery by Missiaglia or Nardi (see pp. 108–109), have your photograph taken surrounded by pigeons (buy some seed from the hawkers to attract them), or go and sit at a table in one of the lovely little rooms in the café Florian (see p. 39). If you've already worked

up an appetite, go and have lunch opposite, at the restaurant Quadri (see p. 39). In the afternoon, there's nothing quite like a romantic stroll along the Riva degli Schiavoni. When you get to the Ponte della Paglia, pause (for a kiss?) in front of the Ponte dei Sospiri (Bridge of Sighs), before sitting at a

café terrace to watch the *vaporetti* plying their way along the canal. The walk along the quayside can take you a fair way to

### QUIET WALKS IN OUT-OF-THE-WAY PLACES

If you prefer quieter districts and peaceful, romantic little *calle* and *campi*, make for the heart of the *sestiere* of Castello, in the neighbourhood of the church of Santa Maria dei Miracoli (see p. 61), a small, pretty church where young Venetians come to get

married. Carry on as far as Cannaregio and stroll along the *fondamenta* dei Mori (see p. 63) as far as the Fondamente Nuove, where you'll have a view of the lagoon. On the other side of the Grand Canal, the Dorsoduro district is full of idyllic places – the Campo San Barnaba, which is very picturesque (see p. 52), the Campo di Santa Margherita (see p. 52) and the Zattere, where you can have an ice cream.

the welcoming benches of the peaceful Giardini Pubblici, on the borders of the *sestiere* of Castello.

### A LOVERS' EVENING

If you haven't managed to get tickets for the Malibran (see p. 119), the Goldoni (see p. 119) or a concert, go and have a quiet candlelit dinner at the Danieli (see p. 59), La Caravella (see p. 76)

or among the modern paintings of the Alla Colomba (see p. 76). Then it will be time for the highlight of the evening – a ride in a gondola (choose a gondolier with a powerful voice if you want to enjoy a serenade). This will take you under the Bridge of Sighs or set you down like guests of honour at Palazzo Vendramin, the winter casino (p. 123). To round off the evening, you have the choice of a Bellini at Harry's Bar (see p. 82), an ombra at Vino Vino (p. 121) or a drink at the Martini Scala (p. 122), the smart disco of the restaurant Antico Martini. All that will then be left for you to do is to return to your luxury hotel and gaze at the stars from the window of your room.

# THE CARNIVAL AND REGATTA

## FESTIVAL FOLLY

The city of the Doges has always been keen on parading and showing off. The Carnival, the regatta, Ascension Day and the Festival of the Redeemer are colourful events that are almost worth a visit in themselves.

## THE CARNIVAL

This takes place over the ten days preceding Shrove Tuesday (the first fortnight in February), when it becomes impossible to find a room without reserving several months in advance. Is is so busy that sometimes you can't even reach the city by road!

The Venice Carnival started in the 10th or 11th century and had its heyday in the 17th century. At that time, the festivities lasted nearly half a year, from October to Lent. The wearing of masks blurred the sexes, negated social differences and allowed every folly. It was forbidden to forbid, and Casanovas threw eggshells filled with perfume under ladies' windows. Others, who were far more subversive, organised balls in the convents. The Carnival was suspended in 1797, at the end of the Republic, and wasn't started again until 1979, at the instigation of an association of Venetians. At first, in the early 1980s, it was spontaneous and inventive. But it was such a huge success that the tourists began to arrive in droves. The Venetians have gradually abandoned the congested *calle* to the foreigners and withdrawn to the heart of the palaces and theatres. It's there, and in certain *campi* far removed from Piazza San Marco, that the Carnival comes into its own.

## THE FESTA DELLA SENSA

On Ascension Day (*Sensa*), a notable of the city perpetuates the Doges' custom of throwing a gold ring and laurel wreath into the water as a token of union with the sea. The following Sunday is the day of the *Vogalonga*, an endurance race involving

Procession in Piazza San Marco *by Bellini (1470)*.

hundreds of boats. The 30km/ 19 mile race from Venice to Burano and back again via the Cannaregio canal is cheered wildly by the waiting crowds.

### THE FESTA DEL REDENTORE

The Festival of the Redeemer, which commemorates the end of the plague of 1576, takes place in the third week in July. You can then reach the island of the Giudecca by means of a bridge formed by a number of boats and see a marvellous firework display.

### THE REGATA STORICA

The historic regatta, which is held on the first Sunday in September, has taken place since the 12th century. Spectators gather on the banks of the Grand Canal and on the

---

PRESENT-DAY HOLIDAYS

(when shops and monuments close)
- **1 Jan.** New Year's Day
- **6 Jan.** Epiphany
- **Late Mar.-early Apr.** Easter Monday
- **25 Apr**. St Mark's Day (patron saint of the city) and anniversay of the Liberation of 1945
- **1 May** Labour Day
- **31 May** *Festa della Sensa* (Ascension Day)
- **15 Aug**. Assumption
- **1 Nov.** All Saints' Day
- **21 Nov.** *Festa della Madonna della Salute* (Festival of the Salute)
- **8 Dec.** *Immacolata* (Immaculate Conception)
- **25 Dec.** Christmas
- **26 Dec.** St. Stephen's Day

---

Ponte Rialto and Ponte dell'Accademia to watch the boat procession. Then it's time for the highlight of the festival, the two-oar gondola race, which arouses the passion of the crowds.

### THE FESTA DELLA MADONNA DELLA SALUTE

Every 21 November, in memory of a vow made during the plague epidemic of 1631, a procession of the faithful sets off from the Basilica San Marco, crosses the floating

bridge built for the occasion over the Grand Canal, and makes its way to S. Maria della Salute to ask the Virgin to keep them in good health.

# THE COMMEDIA DELL'ARTE

## CARNIVAL MASKS AND COSTUMES

The Carnival (from *carne vale*, meaning, literally, 'farewell to the flesh') has become one of the most important events in the Venetian cultural calendar. Throughout the year, countless mask makers and costume sellers can supply you with everything you need to play a part in the ten-day festival preceding Lent.

## HOW A MASK IS MADE

The mask maker first shapes the mask out of clay, then pours plaster into it to make a mould. This fragile plaster shell is lined with papier mâché (a mixture of paper, rags and glue) and left to dry. After removing the mask from the mould, the craftsman polishes its surface and carefully finishes it, which involves cutting out the eyes, mouth, etc. A coat of white primer is then applied to the mask, which is finally painted by hand.

## LEATHER MASKS

These are far more expensive than papier mâché masks and can take a variety of forms (characters of the Commedia dell'Arte, double masks, Baroque masks in the form of the sun or the moon, etc.). The mask maker softens the leather to shape it, then covers it in gold leaf and colours it according to his choice.

## CARNIVAL ELEGANCE: *TAROCCO* AND *MASCHERA NOBILE*

*Tarocco* outfits are reminiscent of the tarot cards used in fortune telling. They're the favourite costumes of Venetians and elegant tourists alike. However, they're closely followed in the popularity stakes by the

*maschera nobile,* the Carnival outfit of aristocrats in the 18th century. This is

made up of the traditional *bauta* (a white mask that appeared in the late 18th century), the *tabarro* (a short cape) and the famous black cocked hat.

## THE CHARACTERS OF THE COMMEDIA DELL'ARTE

Each of the stock characters of the Commedia dell'Arte was the incarnation of a human vice or form of ridicule. They were immediately recognisable to the audience by their silhouettes and masks (the female characters – Colombine, Isabella and Silvia – didn't wear masks). The following are the main costumes you'll come across in the streets of Venice during the Carnival.

**Harlequin**: Pantalone's valet, Arlecchino, wears a diamond-patterned outfit (red, orange and green) and a black mask. He was originally coarse and cynical before becoming a comical acrobat and, later, in the works of Marivaux, a naive, sensitive servant.

**Brighella**: Pantalone's manservant and the personification of treachery, Brighella uses and abuses stratagems to achieve his ends. He wears a white costume with diagonal green stripes and a green mask with a broken nose that makes him look rather frightening.

**The Doctor**: il Dottore is a lawyer and a typical man of letters; he's both talkative and pretentious. He wears knee-stockings, black breeches and a black cape over a white shirt and ruff; his mask has a prominent forehead and a big nose.

**Pantalone**: an old skinflint who's also passionately in love; he's the favourite butt of the servants' jokes. He wears black trousers and a mask with a moustache embellished with a long hooked nose.

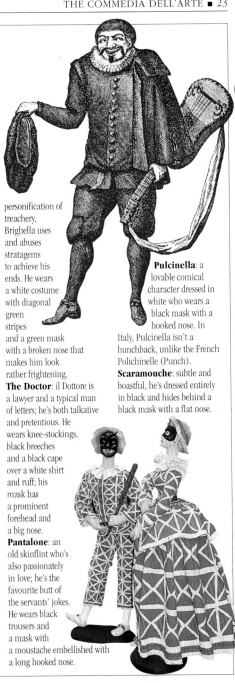

**Pulcinella**: a lovable comical character dressed in white who wears a black mask with a hooked nose. In Italy, Pulcinella isn't a hunchback, unlike the French Polichinelle (Punch).

**Scaramouche**: subtle and boastful, he's dressed entirely in black and hides behind a black mask with a flat nose.

# THE FINER POINTS OF LACEMAKING

## VENETIAN *MERLETTI*

One fine day, a long-haul sailor gave his love a strange marine plant, *Halynedia opuntia*, which is more commonly known as 'mermaids' lace'. When he had left, the young woman did her best to reproduce the plant using only her needle. She thus invented the *punto in aria* (needlepoint), which is derived from the technique for making fishing nets. Today, only a handful of Burano lacemakers are willing to 'ruin their eyesight' with the true art of Venetian *merletto*. The rest is just embroidery.

## BURANO LACE AND VENETIAN LACE

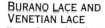

Venetian lace is a linen fabric made with a needle (*ad ago*) rather than a bobbin (*a fuseli*). The background and the flowers, or *ornements,* are formed by the lacemaker over a paper pattern fixed to a cushion. This *punto in aria* (needlepoint), invented around 1540, first involves the construction of a grid or framework. It's this that makes all the difference between Venetian *merletto*

and simple embroidery, which requires a foundation to support the work. The lace found in Venice is either Burano lace or Venetian lace. Burano lace is easily recognisable by its background of square stitches and its transparency. It's the most delicate and also the most expensive, and can only be found at Jesurum (see p. 103). Venetian lace, unashamedly copied by the Colbert lace of Bayeux, has a background consisting of brides and bars. It's a play on relief and allows lacemakers to make very complex designs. Along with the bobbin lace made along the coast (at Chioggia and Pellestrina), this is the best type of lace you can buy in the shops of Burano.

Around 1750, Venice responded by setting up its own factories, but skilled workers became more and more difficult to find. In 1872, only one woman still knew how to make needlepoint lace. It was she who taught in the lacemaking school – *Scuola dei merletti* – which opened in Burano. Nowadays, almost the entire output of the last remaining lacemakers is sold by the shop Jesurum (see p. 103).

## A SHORT HISTORY OF LACEMAKING

Lace has been popular in Venice since the early Middle Ages, and by the 16th century it was no longer reserved for vestments only.

It had also found its way onto blouses and dresses, and later onto men's clothes, fans, sheets, curtains and even shoes. When Louis IV's minister, Colbert, set up a lace factory in France in the 17th century, it dealt a heavy blow to Venetian production as the best Burano lacemakers left the island in answer to his call.

## EMBROIDERY AND COMPUTING

Lacemaking is a very labour-intensive process. A hand-embroidered linen tablecloth represents three years' work and even a simple tablecloth involves the labour of seven women (from design to finishing). All this must be paid for and it doesn't come cheap.

Since the 1980s, computers have helped to bring down the cost of lacemaking. Software has been developed that makes it possible to copy and modify any design. The designs are transferred to cards, stored in memory and executed by machines that can do the equivalent of a day's work by hand in less than an hour. You can find the 'machine embroidery' produced in this way (made in Taiwan or Singapore) on sale at tempting prices in the shops of Burano.

# MURANO GLASS AND GLASS-MAKERS
## TRANSPARENCY AND COLOUR

From the Renaissance to the great figures of the 20th century, including Archimede Seguso, Ermanno Toso, Ercole Barovier and Paolo Venini, the master glass-makers of Murano have ceased to develop and improve an art that remains forever linked with the name of Venice. Read on to learn a little more about the famous Murano glass.

## THE HISTORY OF MURANO GLASS

Glass has been made in Venice since as long ago as the 10th century, but it only took off with the arrival of Byzantine craftsmen following the sack of Constantinople in 1204. The Doges soon moved the guild's kilns to the island of Murano. Officially, this was to protect the city from fire. What is more certain is that

the Serenissima was seeking to protect itself from competition. Its master glass-makers were forbidden to

share their secrets or further foreign initiatives in any way whatsoever. Offenders immediately had their property confiscated and could even be sentenced to death. In the 15th and 16th centuries, master glass-makers invented coloured glass and refined their techniques. They created new shapes of vase, and designed chandeliers and mirrors. Venetian production began to show signs of decline in the 17th century, when it

was faced with competition from Bohemian glass, and later, in the 19th century, with the success of crystal.

## MURANO GLASS-MAKING

Various ingredients are used to obtain the vitrifiable raw material based on siliceous sand or silica (70% of the mixture by weight). The mixture is heated to 1,400°C/2500°F, before the temperature is lowered to 1,000°C/1800°F to allow the glass-blower to carry out his work. On the end of a hollow rod, he picks up some molten glass and places it in a mould to obtain a ball. He blows briefly down the rod and turns it rapidly in order to prevent the ball at the end from stretching. After pinching the base, he blows again before

### THE MAIN TYPES OF MURANO GLASS

**Aventurine**
translucent brown glass with inclusions of very brilliant copper crystals.

*Cristallino*
glass resembling rock crystal made from silica and manganese. This technique, which was invented by the master glass-maker Angelo Barovier (1405–1460), made the Murano glass famous.

*Lattimo*
glass that imitates porcelain (*porcellana contraffatta*) whose opacity is due to the addition of tin oxide; the designation *lattimo* also covers colourless glass with white inclusions.

*Millefiori*
the assemblage of various pieces of coloured glass to create a design; the whole thing is then melted in order to make the pieces stick together.

**Lead glass**
inexpensive glass that's far softer than the *cristallino* type; it's used to do enamel work and to make the lengths of beading from which Murano beads are made.

**Lace-glass**
a technique invented in 1527; coloured or enamelled straws are included in colourless molten glass.

*Ghiaccio* **glass**
a technique invented around 1570 where frozen water is added to the vitrified paste; the thermal difference creates an undulating pattern that gives the glass the appearance of melted ice.

**Cut glass**
glass with (often floral) designs drawn with diamond tips.

piercing the ball with a sharp point. He then shapes the glass to give it its curved form. Once this is complete, the glass is again heated before being placed in a kiln kept at a lower temperature.

# GILDED WOOD AND MIRRORS
## GOLDEN REFLECTIONS

The whole of Europe has long admired the furniture and mirrors made by the Venetian cabinetmakers and Murano glass-makers. Resplendent with Baroque gilding, Chinese laquer and translucent colours, these works of art form an integral part of the Venetian landscape.

from Bassano. This type of mirror is also well represented in the large antique shops, and the shops on Murano sell more or less successful modern copies of them.

## MIRRORS

The oldest mirrors you'll see in the palaces date from the 16th century. They have heavy walnut frames and resemble small altarpieces. In the following century they acquired cut-glass pediments that were often blue in colour. Mirrors with a gilded wooden frame flourished in the 18th century, when Rococo was all the rage. This type of mirror, with its ornate moulding using a theme of plants, can be found (along with 19th-

century pastiches) in the large antique shops of the city, but they cost a fortune. One of them fetched the sum of £35,000 at auction in 1987. In the late 18th century, wooden moulding covered in gold leaf gradually disappeared, except on mirrors destined for the decoration of the great palaces. From then on, the borders were made of engraved glass, decorated with spun glass, colourful Murano glass flowers and polychrome earthenware

## VENETIAN FURNITURE

It was in Venice that the finest Italian furniture of the 18th century was produced.

In style, it was Louis XV, Louis XVI or Chippendale (Rococo enriched with designs influenced by Chinese, Japanese or Gothic art).

Most of this furniture was made of lacquered walnut decorated with floral motifs. Here are some of the most notable pieces.

**The pedestal desk:**
a desk whose upper part acts as a small bookcase; the Venetian vogue for this item of furniture can be explained by the importance of writing and printing in the city.

**The chair:**
*the* great speciality of the cabinetmakers of the Serenissima; Venetian chairs can be

**The sofa:**
an Italian invention (17th-century). The sofa took on vast proportions in Venice as elsewhere; the finest had openwork embroidery backs (these sofas are valued at around £10,000).

**The chest of drawers:**
pot-bellied as the period required, they were lacquered a pale shade and decorated with Rococo motifs.

**The armchair:**
its originality resided in its three carved walnut feet; some armchairs that were lacquered and embellished with precious reliefs were works of art.

**The console table:**
with its undulating top surmounted by a

distinguished from their English models by the caning and the use of Chinese or Japanese lacquers.

## HOW TO TELL THE REAL FROM THE FAKE

Check the hinges carefully (they're always imperfect because they're handmade), as well as the roughness of the inner surfaces (wood was once always sawn by hand). Check that old parts haven't been combined with new, artificially aged ones. Finally, look out for that classic – woodworm imitated with buckshot. You should scarcely be able to get a needle in the hole (the tunnel dug by a worm is winding, not straight).

Murano glass mirror, it was used as a tidy by the nobles.

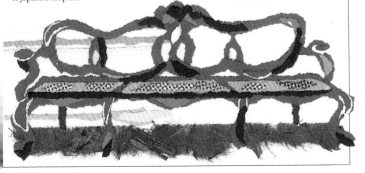

# THE FLAVOURS OF VENICE
## 1001 TEMPTING TASTES

Venetian cuisine has its roots in a dual tradition based on both land and sea. It draws on the riches of the Adriatic and the islands of the lagoon, where a multitude of vegetables grow. This leads to an unusual blend of flavours. Fish, shellfish and waterfowl are prepared with consummate skill, and there are delicate pastries, too.

### VENETIAN CUISINE

The writers of the past, starting with Goldoni and Casanova, mentioned Venetian cuisine and alluded to its Oriental aspect and spicy, sweet-and-sour (*al agro*) flavours. Olive oil, onions, rice, almonds, pine nuts and dried fruit are its recurring themes. Although it's filling, it's also extremely healthy thanks to a wide variety of market-garden produce (peas, beans, asparagus, artichokes, endives, courgettes).

### POLENTA

This grilled corn bread, which is usually yellow in colour, but sometimes white, is the main accompaniment to a large number of Venetian dishes. It's very easy to make. For 3 people, add 250gm/8oz of cornflour to a litre/1³/₄pt of boiling salted water and cook for 30 mins (or more, for an even better flavour), stirring the mixture the whole time. Pour into a greased mould and leave to cool. Cut into rectangles and brown under a grill.

## SOME TYPICALLY VENETIAN DISHES

These local dishes and desserts feature less often on restaurant menus than the basics mentioned on p. 30. If you come across them in a restaurant, don't miss the opportunity of trying them – they'll be a real treat for the taste buds.

*A box of amarettos is easy to bring back.*

### ■ Starters

*Brodo di pesce:* a delicious saffron-flavoured fish soup.
*Fiori di Zucchini:* courgette-flower fritters stuffed with fish mousse.
*Risi e bisi:* a pea and rice-based dish (sometimes flavoured with bacon).
*Risotto alle seppie:* rice with parmesan and cuttlefish ink.

### ■ Vegetables

*Fagioli in saor:* large marinated beans.
*Melanzane in saor:* marinated aubergines.
*Pappardelle col radicchio:* broad pasta with red Treviso endives grilled in oil with onions and garlic.

### ■ Pasta

*Bigoli in salsa:* a kind of thick wholemeal spaghetti cooked in an onion and anchovy sauce.
*Spaghetti ai carciofi:* spaghetti with artichokes.

### ■ Meat and fish

*Anguilla in umido:* eel in tomato sauce with white wine and garlic.

*Braciola alla veneziana:* breaded pork chops cooked in white wine vinegar.
*Seppie in tecia:* cuttlefish in white wine with tomato and basil.

### ■ Sweets

*Amaretti:* small almond-flavoured cakes to eat with coffee.

*Baute:* colourful chocolates that are found all over the city.
*Croccantini:* nougat eaten with sweet wine in bistrots.
*Essi buranelli:* S-shaped egg

biscuits (when ring-shaped, they're known as *bussolai buranelli*).

*Galani:* small cakes that are fried and sprinkled with sugar; they're eaten at Carnival time and are also called *crostoli*.
*Tiramisù:* a delicious cake made from biscuits sprinkled with amaretto, and almond and coffee-flavoured mascarpone, all sprinkled with chocolate.
*Zaeti:* small cornflour rolls sprinkled with icing sugar.

### IN SAOR

You'll often come across the words *in saor* in restaurants. They usually appear in conjunction with vegetables (beans, or *fagioli*) and fish (the well-known *sarde*, or sardines *in saor*). This marinade, consisting of white wine vinegar, onions, pine nuts and raisins, was once used to keep produce fresh. Sailors used to take it with them on long voyages to prevent them from getting scurvy.

# THE WINES AND SPIRITS OF VENETIA
## BARDOLINO, VALPOLICELLA AND GRAPPA

Venetia produces eleven DOC (*Denominazione di origine controllata,* or appellation contrôlée) wines and a countless number of local (IGT, or *Indicazione Tipica*) wines and table wines. To these must be added all the many varieties of *grappa,* or brandy, made from the best wines of the region.

## THE WINE REGIONS

The Venetian wines come from the Verona region (around Lake Garda) and Vicenze (west of Venice), or north of Treviso (the Piave valley). They represent 13% of the entire wine production of Italy, putting Venetia in third place behind Sicily and Apulia.

## THE WINES OF THE VERONA REGION: BARDOLINO, SOAVE AND VALPOLICELLA

These are the best wines of Venetia. They're exported abroad in vast quantities and wine lovers will almost certainly be familiar with them. They come from the shores of Lake Garda north-west of Verona.

**Bardolino** (a small town on the south-east of Lake Garda) wine comes as either *chiaretto* (rosé) or *classico* (red). It's marvellous chilled with meat and cheese.

**Soave** *classico* is a smooth, fairly robust white wine that goes well with white meat and fish. It's the fourth most exported Italian wine.

**Valpolicella** (the fifth most exported Italian wine) is a full-bodied red. It can be drunk at room temperature or chilled. It comes in two forms: Valpolicella *classico* or, better still, Valpolicella *superiore.*

### *The other labels*

The Verona region produces three other appellation contrôlée wines that you can try:

**Bianco du Custoza,** a white wine that should be drunk chilled with meals or as an aperitif.

**Gambellara,** a light, dry wine (red or white).

**Valdadige** (red, rosé or white), which is produced on the banks of the Adige.

## THE TREVISO REGION

The best wine of the region is **Prosecco**, a sparkling wine (very dry, dry or medium dry) produced from the vines on the hills of Conegliano and Valdobbiadene, north of Treviso. The Venetians drink it as an aperitif. Those in the know swear by the Prosecco of Cartizze, which has the richest flavour. Prosecco also exists in the form of a classic white wine and a *frizzante*.

### *The other labels*

Other wines of the Treviso region have been designated DOC (appellation contrôlée):

**Colli di Conegliano,** a smooth, very robust red or white wine.

**Montello e Colli Asolani,** red, white, or *spumante* with a hint of almonds.

**Piave,** red or white, but the least good and held in low esteem by wine connoisseurs.

## WINE TERMS

*Amabile:* medium dry
*Bianco:* white
*Classico:* standard quality
*Frizzante:* slightly sparkling
*Rosso:* red
*Secco:* dry
*Spumante:* sparkling
*Superiore:* superior quality

## GRAPPA

Brandy, or *grappa*, (around 40°) is produced throughout northern Italy. A little drop in your coffee (order a *coretto)* will set you

up to explore the city. In Venetia, the best *grappa* is made from Prosecco or Valpolicella.

## WHERE TO TASTE AND BUY WINE

If you want to taste the Venetian wines, go to an *osteria-enoteca*:
Al Volto (p. 121),
Da Aciugheta (p. 59),
Do Mori (p. 55)
or Vino Vino (p. 121).
If you want to buy some wine, see the places listed on pp. 98–99.

## APERITIFS AND LIQUEURS

If you want to try one of the strange-tasting aperitifs that are so typically Italian, order a spritz with Aperol (which is made from oranges), Cynar (which is artichoke-flavoured and very bitter) or that old favourite, Campari. The great liqueurs of the region are Amaretto (which is almond-flavoured, 24–28°, and made from apricot stones) and Amari (a bitter liqueur that's around 45° made from the bark and roots of various plants).

# Venice Practicalities

## GETTING ABOUT

You can get about by *vaporetto* or *motoscafo*. *Vaporetti* are large and fairly slow, and offer great views of Venice from their open decks. *Motoscafi* sit low in the water and are faster, with small decks. You can use them to get to the islands of the lagoon (Murano, Burano and Torcello).

The *motonave*, a kind of big ferry-steamer, only serves the parts of Venice where cars are allowed, including the Lido.

## THE MOST USEFUL LINES

The most useful lines (maps are available from the tourist information office) and their most useful stops are:

**1**: Piazzale Roma-Ferrovia-Rialto-S. Marco-Lido (and vice versa).

**12**: F. Nuove-Murano-Burano-Torcello-Treporti.

**13**: F. Nuove-Murano-Vignole-Treporti.

**14**: S. Zaccaria-Lido-Punta Sabbioni.

**52**: Piazzale Roma-Ferrovia-F. Nuove-Bacini-Lido-S. Zaccaria-Zattere-P. Roma..

**82**: S. Zaccaria-Piazzale Roma-Tronchetto-Redentore-Giudecca-S. Giorgio-S. Zaccaria.

A line through a number means that the *vaporetto* only runs on part of the line.

## DEPARTURE TIMES

In general, you have to wait 10 minutes for a *vaporetto* between 7am and 9.30pm, 20 minutes between 9.30pm and 12.30am and 20 minutes to an hour for lines that run all night (lines 1, 12 and 82 on at least part of their routes).

## TICKETS

You can buy these from the ticket offices of major stations (fares are displayed and vary according to the journey), as well as kiosks and tobacconists' displaying the initials ACTV. Buy your tickets from them in advance because they cost considerably more on board.

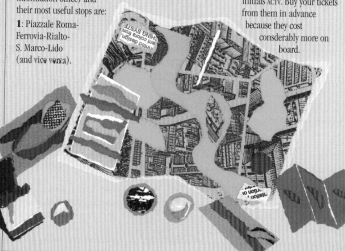

## 24-HOUR AND 3-DAY TICKETS

Both the 24-hour ticket (L18,000) and the 3-day ticket (L30,000) are ideal for flying visits and will save you money if you make three or more journeys a day. Valid for most journeys, they can be bought at the same places as ordinary tickets.
For further information, contact the ACTV office in Piazzale Roma, open every day 7.30am-8pm ☎ 041 528 78 86.

## TRAGHETTI

Aboard spartan gondolas and for next to nothing, you can cross the Grand Canal in seven places (from morning to evening, at the yellow signs):
S. M. del Giglio, S. Barnaba, S. Tomà, Carbon, S. Sofia, S. Marcuola and Ferrovia.

## GONDOLAS

A gondola ride will cost you around L100,000 for 50 minutes (up to 6 people) and L45,000 for every 25 minutes extra.
It's a good idea to agree on the price in advance and worth bargaining for a reduction, especially out of season.
There are 12 gondola 'ranks'. The best are: S. M. del Giglio, S. Marco, S. Toma and Rialto.

## TAXI ACQUEI

In the historic centre, a short ride aboard one of these varnished wooden speedboats, from Piazzale Roma to the city centre, will cost you approximately L80,000, maybe more. Prices vary greatly according to the journey and the boatman. Try bargaining.

### Taxi rank telephones:
Piazzale Roma
☎ 041 71 69 22 ;
Rialto ☎ 041 523 05 75 ;
S. Marco ☎ 041 522 97 50.

Taxi-boats can be reserved from:
Coop. Veneziana
☎ 041 71 61 24 ;
Coop. Serenissima
☎ 041 522 12 65.

# MAKING A PHONE CALL

There are plenty of telephones about (taking cards, coins and tokens). The only

problem is that you have to use a lighter to be able to dial the number at night.
There are 3 kinds of cards (L5, 10 and 15,000). A card machine can be found at the Fondaco dei Tedeschi post office (Salizzada Fondacco dei Tedeschi, 929, Cannaregio) if the tobacconists' (look for the black 'T' sign) have sold out (which is often the case in the city centre). Before using the card, break off the corner marked with a dotted line.
You can phone from SIP (Italian Telecom) offices, for example, the one near the Fondaco dei Tedeschi (every day except Sunday, 8.30am-7.30pm). You pay at the till.

## HOW TO FIND AN ADDRESS

In Venice, an address is made up of a figure followed by the name of the district (S. Marco, Dorsoduro, S. Polo, S. Croce, Cannaregio, Castello, Giudecca, etc.). It's disconcerting at first, but you soon get used to it. Go to the district in question and ask a passer-by for more precise directions. You then simply follow the numbers round to the correct place. If you want to find your way more quickly, you can buy the *Indicatore Anagrafico* (from a bookshop), which gives the names of the streets corresponding to the various numbers.

To telephone abroad, dial 00 followed by the country code, (Aus 61, NZ 64, Canada/USA 1, UK 44, Ireland 353) then the number you require. Since 1998, local numbers in Italy have to be dialled as if you were calling from outside the town or city. This means that all the numbers given in this guidebook need to be preceded by 041 – the code for Venice – unless another code is given in the case of more distant towns. When calling Venice from abroad, the country code for Italy is 39, followed by 041 and the number in Venice.

## CHANGING MONEY

The banks open every day except Saturday and Sunday, 8.30am-1.30pm, 3.35-4.35pm.
There are many cash machines (taking Visa and Eurocard) in the Mercerie, Strada Nuova and Calle Larga XXII Marzo. A bureau de change stays open late in Piazza S. Marco (high commission charged). For American Express card holders:
Calle Larga XXII Marzo, 1471 S. Marco ☎ 041 520 08 44 (9am-5.30pm).

## SENDING A LETTER OR POSTCARD

You can buy stamps from tobacconists' or post offices. You need a L750 stamp for a letter to a country in the European Union. The letterboxes are usually red (national and international mail) but sometimes blue (international mail).

**Main post office**:
Fondaco dei Tedeschi (Salizzada Fondaco dei Tedeschi, 929 Cannaregio ☎ 041 271 71 11 (8.30am-7pm).

## TOURIST INFORMATION OFFICES

These are open every day except Sunday, 8.30am-7.30pm (opening times vary according to season), and can be found in various parts of the city:
Palazzetto (near the Giardini Reali) and Calle dell'Ascensione (under the arcades of the Procuratie Nuove).
Stazione S. Lucia (8am-7pm)
☎ and 🖷 041 71 90 78.

Viale S. M. Elisabetta, Lido
☎ 041 526 57 21,
🖷 041 529 87 20.

Central switchboard:
☎ 041 529 87 11.

You can get a map of the city here, as well as a plan of the *vaporetto* network and the indispensable monthly publication *Un Ospite di Venezia* (in Italian and English), which lists exhibitions, concerts and plays and provides lots of practical information, including the opening times of the city's major monuments. If you come on the spur of the moment, they'll also reserve you a hotel room.

# OPENING TIMES

## MUSEUMS AND MONUMENTS

Opening times vary enormously from place to place and from season to season. The best way to find out when a particular place is open is to read *Un Ospite di Venezia*. As a rough guide, the famous monuments and big museums open from 9/10am to 4pm or even 6/7pm, and small museums and private museums from 9am to 1pm. Monday is often, but not always, closing day.

## CHURCHES

In general, these are open every morning until noon, then again from 4.30 to 7pm. Some only open for mass or remain permanently closed, for no apparent reason.

## SHOPS

These open every day except Sunday 9/9.30am-1.30pm and 3.30/4pm-7.30pm. Tourist shops (selling masks, Murano glass, etc.) don't close in the middle of the day. They also open on Sundays in season and at Carnival time.

# FINDING OUT

The *Gazzettino* and *Nuova Venezia* are the two Venetian dailies. They contain useful information (duty chemist's, weather forecast, etc.) and cinema and theatre programmes. Look, too, at the luxurious cultural monthly, *Marco Polo* (in English and Italian), that every lover of Venice will want to buy.

## USEFUL PHONE NUMBERS

### AIRPORT

**Marco Polo Airport:**
☎ 041 260 61 11.

**General information:**
☎ 041 260 92 60.

**Lost property:**
☎ 041 260 64 36.

### AIR COMPANIES

**Alitalia (at Marco Polo Airport):**
☎ 041 260 9260

**British Airways Customer Service in Rome:**
☎ 06 650 11413

### SANTA LUCIA RAILWAY STATION

**Information:**
☎ 041 14 78 88 088.

**Lost property:**
☎ 041 78 52 38.

### CAR PARKS

**Isola del Tronchetto:**
☎ 041 520 75 55.

**Piazzale Roma:**
☎ 041 520 62 35.

**Other car parks:** Punta Sabbioni and Treporti (14 vaporetto), as well as Mestre-Fusina and Mestre-S. Giuliano in season (frequent trains to Venice-S. Lucia, 2, 4, 7 and 12 buses to Venezia-Piazzale Roma).

### LOST CREDIT CARDS

**American Express:**
☎ 06 7 22 82.

**Mastercard:**
☎ 16 78 6 80 86.

**Visa:**
☎ 16 78 21 00 1
or ☎ 1678 220 56 to have any card blocked.

### EMERGENCIES

**Ospedale Civile:**
Campo S. Giovanni e Polo
☎ 041 523 00 00.

**Emergencies:**
☎ 113.

**Police:**
☎ 112.

**Ambulance:**
☎ 523 00 00.

**Fire:**
☎ 115.

**Vehicle breakdown (ACI):**
☎ 116.

**Night chemists':**
For a complete list, see *Un Ospite di Venezia* or the daily newspapers *La Nuova Venezia* and *Il Gazzettino*.

### CONSULATES AND EMBASSIES

**British Consulate:**
☎ 041 522 7207
US, Irish, Canadian, Australian and New Zealand embassies are all in Rome.

### PLACES OF WORSHIP

**St Mark's Basilica:**
Piazza S. Marco
☎ 041 522 56 97
Sunday Mass at 7am, 8am, 9am, 10am (in Latin), 11.30am, 12.30pm and 6.45pm.
And in the churches of Venice.

**Synagogue:**
Ghetto Vecchio
☎ 041 71 50 12.
Sat. at 9.30am and Fri. at 5pm.

**Lutheran Evangelical Church:**
Campo S.S. Apostoli, 4443
☎ 041 524 20 40.

**Orthodox Church:**
Ponte dei Greci, 3412 Castello
☎041 522 54 46
Sun. at 11am and 12noon.

# Piazza San Marco:
## the cradle of the city

## Sestiere di San Marco

**M**assive monuments, luxury shops on every side, crowds mingling with flocks of pigeons and the endless clicking of cameras all make this 'Europe's finest drawing-room', as Napoleon once described it. You can visit this display of splendour several times and never tire of it. In the early dawn light, at sunset or by night, the Piazza San Marco is more fascinating than ever.

### ❶ Piazza San Marco★★★

The vast St. Mark's Square, the most famous attraction in Venice, is the only square

in the city to be graced with the title *piazza*, so-called because the Venetians wanted to mark its importance in the city compared to the other *campi*.

### ❷ Basilica San Marco★★★

**Every day 9.30am-4.30pm in winter, 5pm in summer**
☎ 041 522 56 97
**Entry charge for galleria**
☎ 041 522 52 05, Pala d'oro and treasury.

The *chiesa d'oro* (golden church), squat and glittering with some 4,000m²/ 4,800sq. yd of mosaics, dates from the 11th century. Among the countless art objects it contains, don't miss the *Pala d'oro*, a gold altarpiece encrusted with 80 enamels and 3,000 precious stones. In addition, don't forget to climb up to the gallery, just to see the square between the hooves of San Marco's famous horses (copies, but still impressive).

## **5** Torre dell'Orologio★★
**Closed for restoration**
☎ 041 523 18 79.

The bell tower is decorated with the signs of the Zodiac and the lion of St Mark, and crowned with two statues of Moors who strike the hours on a large bell.

## **6** Piazzetta★★

With its gondolas moored to the quayside and the island of San Giorgio Maggiore in the distance, this 'little square' presents one of the most photogenic landscapes in Venice. The two columns, surmounted by a winged lion, the symbol of St Mark, and by St Theodore, the first patron saint of the city, were brought back from the Orient.

## **7** Quadri★★
**Piazza San Marco, 120**
☎ 041 522 21 05
**Every day 9am-midnight.**

The indispensable counterpart to the Florian (opened in 1775),

## **8** FLORIAN★★★
**Piazza San Marco 56-59 (San Marco)**
☎ 041 520 56 41
**Every day except Wed. 9am-midnight.**

You can't possibly come to Venice without having a drink in one of Florian's cosy little rooms. The café opened in 1720 and is a real gem. It was once the meeting-place of artists and poets, and many famous people have been here before you. Come back time and again to sample all the pastries and get to know every part of it. You'll get a charming welcome, too.

with decor only slightly less chic and delightful, an equally hushed atmosphere and comparably high prices. The price of drinks inevitably goes up when the orchestra's playing, across the piazza.

## **3** Campanile★★
**Entry charge (lift)**
**Every day 9.30am-3.30pm in winter, 9/10pm in summer**
☎ 041 522 40 64
**Entry charge.**

The campanile collapsed without warning in 1912, but luckily the only victim was a cat, and it was soon rebuilt exactly as before. The view of Venice from the top is a must.

## **4** Palazzo Ducale★★★
**Every day 9am-5.30pm in winter, 7pm in summer**
☎ 041 522 49 51
**Entry charge (ticket office closes an hour earlier).**

In this marvel of Gothic architecture (1340–1424), each room is more beautiful than the last. Some are decorated by Veronese, others by Tintoretto, who created the largest oil painting in the world for the Grand Council Chamber, *Vision of Paradise* (22m/72ft by 7m/23ft).

# The Fenice district:
## churches, canals and luxury shops

The district dotted with churches and streaked with canals and quiet *campi* between Piazza San Marco and Teatro la Fenice is where most of Venice's smartest shops, some of its best antique dealers and other well-known galleries can be found. Such a display of luxury isn't within the reach of all, but you can always indulge in a little window-shopping.

*[Map labels: R. dei Fuseri; Rio della Verona; C. d. Verona; R. dei Barcaroli; C. d. Barca d. Frezzeria; C. della FANTIN Fenice; C.S. Fruttarol; **S. Fantin**; C. Bognolo; Frezzeria; **Museo Correr** (1); **Teatro la Fenice** (8); (7); (5); R. d. Veste; Rio; C. dell'Ascension; R. d. Fenice; C. d. Veste; C. d. Veste; Rio; C.S. S. Moisè; S. S. Moisè; C. dei Vallaresso; **S. Maria del Giglio** (4); Calle Larga 22 Marzo (2); di S. Moisè; **S. Moisè** (3); C. S. M. ZOBENIGO (6); Rio d. Ostreghe; C. d. Traghetto; **Gritti Palace**; Canal Grande]*

A slightly dusty museum that traces the important events in Venice's history. The art gallery has an impressive collection of paintings, and not only Venetian ones. Along with two or three fine Bellinis, there's a sublime *Pietà* by Antonello da Messina that's worth a look.

## ❶ Museo Correr★★★
Piazza San Marco, 52
☎ 041 522 56 25
Every day 9am-5pm in winter, 7pm in summer
Entry charge.

## ❷ Calle Larga XXII Marzo★

The smartest street in Venice and home to the great names in fashion, leather goods and high-quality souvenirs. Visitors will never tire of walking up and down here (and in its extension, the Salizada San Moisè and the little Calle Vallaresso). The buildings are impressive, and even the banks look like monuments.

## ❸ Church of San Moisè★
Every day 3.30-7pm
☎ 041 528 58 40.

The Venetians must have been short of saints to venerate when they canonised Moses

> CALLE LARGA
> XXII MARZO

THE FENICE DISTRICT **2** 41

and dedicated this church to him in the 17th century. This example of unbridled Baroque stands next to the appalling façade of the Bauer-Grünwald hotel.

### 4 Church and campo of Santa Maria del Giglio★
Church every day 10am-5pm except Sun. morning.
☎ 041 522 57 39.

The *campo* dominated by Santa Maria del Giglio (the Church of the

Lily) is the gondoliers' headquarters. In the evening, it echoes to serenades performed by the men in boaters. Come here to dream of eternal Venice.

### 5 Church of San Fantin★
Every day 7.30am-noon, 4-7pm
☎ 041 523 52 36.

This magnificent white stone Renaissance building is the joint creation of two of Venice's best architects, Scarpagnigno and Sansovino, who built the dome which rests on four impressive Corinthian columns. The nearby *scuola* houses thirteen works by the painter Palma the Younger.

### 6 Hotel Gritti Palace ★★
Campo Santa Maria del Giglio, 2467
☎ 041 794 611.

With its 17th-century furniture, Persian carpets, waterside restaurant and view of the Grand Canal, the Gritti is one of the top ten hotels in the world. The prices are astronomical, of course, but money isn't generally an issue if you come to you stay at the Gritti!

### 7 Al Teatro restaurant★
Campo San Fantin, 1916
☎ 041 522 10 52
Open every day.

One of the two obligatory places to go after a performance at La Fenice (the other is Antico Martini, see p. 76). Opera lovers used to come here (and will again on 1 October 2001) to sample the best cuisine in Venice. If you think it's out of your price range, you can always just buy your cigarettes there, a rare commodity in Venice by night.

### 8 TEATRO LA FENICE★
Campo San Fantin, 2549 San Marco
☎ 041 521 01 61
Closed until Oct. 2001.

One of the oldest opera houses in the world was destroyed by fire in January 1996 and the Venetians were distraught by this devastating loss. However, they've promised that the phoenix will rise once again from the ashes (completed in 1792, La Fenice had already succumbed to the flames once before in 1836). By 1 October 2001, the red and gold auditorium will have been completely rebuilt in its original form and should ring to the arias of Rossini that were first performed here. Future productions are eagerly awaited.

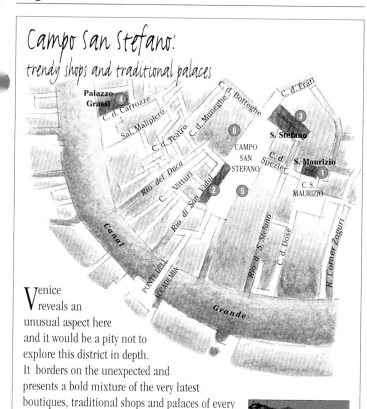

# Campo San Stefano:
## trendy shops and traditional palaces

Venice reveals an unusual aspect here and it would be a pity not to explore this district in depth. It borders on the unexpected and presents a bold mixture of the very latest boutiques, traditional shops and palaces of every period, clustered round a square that's far too large. And all in the shadow of a campanile that looks as if it could collapse at any moment!

### ❶ Campo San Maurizio★

The church of San Maurizio (rebuilt in the 19th century) and the Lombardesque façade of the Scuola degli Albanesi (16th-century) stand in a quiet little *campo* that will leave you with fond memories. The Palazzo Bellavite is also worth a look, although it's lost the Veronese frescoes with which it was once decorated. Venice's second-hand market is held in this charming setting several times a year (see p. 43).

### ❷ Palaces of Campo San Stefano★
**Closed to the public.**

The Campo San Stefano used to be covered with grass, and was used for bullfights until the early 19th century.

Three of the most powerful Venetian families chose this oddly shaped esplanade to build a series of sumptuous palaces – the Loredans in the 16th century, the Morosinis in the 17th century and the Pisanis in the 18th century.

### ❸ Church of San Stefano★

**Every day 8am-7pm, Sun. 10am-8pm**
☎ **041 522 50 61.**

Flanked by a bell tower that leans alarmingly, the church is entered via a remarkable Flamboyant Gothic portal. A few paintings by some of the greatest artists (Vivarini, Palma the Elder and Tintoretto) are housed in the nave and sacristy.

### ❹ Palazzo Grassi★★

**Campo San Samuele, 3231 San Marco**
☎ **041 523 16 80**
**Open only for exhibitions.**

This gigantic palace, built by the Grassi family in 1730, was the last to go up on the Grand Canal. The building, which was sinking dangerously into

the lagoon, was restored in 1986. The car manufacturer, Fiat, which owns the walls, sponsors outstanding exhibitions every year (Marcel Duchamp in 1993, Henry Moore in 1995 and Giambattista Tiepolo in 1996). The café is run by Harry's Bar (see p. 82), which is a sure sign of quality, so you needn't worry about eating there.

### ❺ Fiorellashop★

**Campo San Stefano, 2806 San Marco**
☎ **041 520 92 28**
**Every day except Sun. 10am-1pm, 3-7pm.**

A weird-looking collection of velvet jackets is displayed on hermaphrodite *doges* wearing high heels. Strange, but true. The shop window is in the

image of the stylist Fiorella Mancini, a key figure in the Carnival, whose humour and insolence are reminiscent of Jean-Paul Gaultier.

(see p. 82)

### SECOND-HAND MARKET IN CAMPO SAN MAURIZIO

If you love old objects but despair at the astronomical prices asked by Venetian antique dealers for the slightest knick-knack, there's only one thing to do. Go to the market held several times a year (at Easter, the third weekend in September and the weekend before Christmas) in the Campo San Maurizio. When making a deal, never lose sight of the fact that the Serenissima still remembers a time when it traded with the Orient, so expect some hard bargaining.

### ❻ San Stefano ice-cream parlour★

**Campo San Stefano, 2692 San Marco**
☎ **041 522 55 76**
**Every day except Mon. 8am-midnight in season, 8.30pm out of season Closed Dec.-Jan.**

The home of traditional Venetian ice cream. Whatever you do, don't miss it – it's an institution. The American ice-cream parlour opposite poses no threat to this well-established classic.

# Around Campo Manin:
## craftsmen and antique dealers

Canal Grande

Rio di S. Luca

CAMPO S.LUCA **4**

CAMPO MANIN **1**

**Palazzo Fortuny** **3**

**Palazzo Corner-Spinelli** **5**

C. d. Spezier

C. d. Mandola

Calle Cortesia

C. d. Verona

Rio delle Verona

C. delle Locande

**Palazzo Contarini del Bovolo** **6**

Rio dei Fuseri

**7**

**2**

CAMPO SANT'ANGELO

Rio di S. Angelo

Peaceful canals, antique shops resembling small museums and craftsmen renewing age-old techniques sit side-by-side with baker's shops, local cafés and all sorts of fascinating little places where you can pick up interesting objects without breaking the bank. The passers-by belong to a species that's in danger of vanishing from the *sestiere* of San Marco – believe it or not, they're Venetians and not just artists!

## ❶ Campo Manin★

The centre of Venice isn't just a shoppers' paradise, it

also has 20th-century monuments, such as the *Cassa di Risparmio* (Savings Bank) built in the *campo* in 1968. While it would be unfair to say that the building has been a complete success, it does demonstrate that Venice isn't just a museum city as is too often said. The vast quadrilateral of the Campo Manin bears the name of the Venetian revolutionary who drove out the Austrians and proclaimed the Republic in 1848.

## ❷ Campo Sant'Angelo★

This aristocratic square lined with palaces is a pleasant place to rest before embarking on a shopping expedition in the neighbouring *calle*. The church of San Michele (the archangel), who gave his name to the *campo*, has disappeared. All that remains is a little oratory adorned with a graceful bell tower. The nearby canal and its pretty bridge are also charming.

## ❸ Palazzo Fortuny★★
☎ 041 520 09 95
**Every day except Mon 10am-6pm. Entry charge.**

This pretty palace, also known as the Pesaro degli Orfei (15th-century), displays a few examples of the fabrics to which the Andalusian Mariano Fortuny

Y Madrazo (1871–1949) gave his name (see p. 16). You can find out all about his work here and see a wealth of marvellous and unusual scarves and dresses.

### ❹ Campo San Luca★

In this lively, typically Venetian *campo*, a marble plinth marks the 'navel' of the city. Its other interest is more prosaic – it's home to the café-patisserie Rosa Salva (see p. 100), one of the best places in Venice to sample *fritelle* or a simple *cornetto* of *fior di latte*. Devotees of Aretino (1492-1556) should visit the tomb of Titian's great contemporary in the church of San Luca, a short distance from the *campo*.

### ❺ Palazzo Corner-Spinelli★★
**Closed to the public**
☎ 041 521 64 11.

The house of Rubelli – one of the great names of Venetian fabrics (see p. 90) – needed a head office to match its prestige, and since moving into this fine palace, it has one. The building itself marks a transition in style. No longer entirely Gothic, it isn't yet Renaissance either. However, its purpose hasn't changed. Its former owners, the Spinellis, were themselves merchants who had grown rich on the silk trade.

### ❻ PALAZZO CONTARINI DEL BOVOLO★★

**Open to the public Apr.-Oct. every day 10am-1pm, 2-6pm**
☎ 041 521 75 21.

Renaissance, Gothic or Byzantine – it would take a genius to label this strange 15th-century palace lying off the beaten tourist track, just by Campo Manin. The fact remains that its other name, Palazzo del *Bovolo* (spiral staircase in the Venetian dialect) is entirely appropriate and that it's impossible to confuse it with any other palace in the city. Its quiet little courtyard and lacy openwork staircase are quite irresistible.

### ❼ Vini da Arturo restaurant
**Calle degli Assassini, 3656 San Marco**
**Every day except Sun. 7.30-10pm**
☎ 041 528 69 74.

A tiny but wonderful restaurant frequented by a well-heeled clientele that doesn't mind paying a high price for the legendary fillet steaks and salads. This is easily the best restaurant to eat at when you're visiting the district (no credit cards).

# The Mercerie

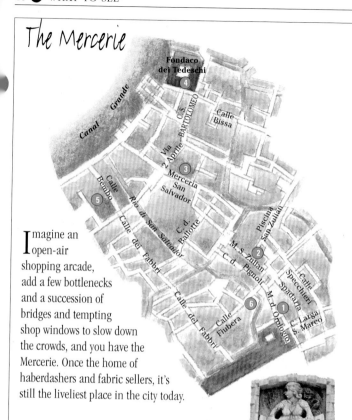

I magine an open-air shopping arcade, add a few bottlenecks and a succession of bridges and tempting shop windows to slow down the crowds, and you have the Mercerie. Once the home of haberdashers and fabric sellers, it's still the liveliest place in the city today.

The shops that line this narrow *calle* are in a different league to those of the *piazza*. Exorbitant jewellers' shops, expensive shoe shops and, here and there, a few stalls offering unusual junk compete with *trattorie* for undemanding tourists.

## ❷ Merceria and church of San Zulian ★★
**Church open irregularly.**

If you get tired of the hustle and bustle of the Merceria, leave the jostling crowds behind you and escape to Campo San

## ❶ Merceria dell'Orologio ★

The Merceria dell'Orologio starts, as its name suggests, under the clock tower of Piazza San Marco (see p. 39).

Zulian. It will seem surprisingly calm and village-like in comparison. The maze of dark alleyways behind the church, in the direction of Santa Maria Formosa (see p. 60), is packed with food shops. Porters shouting *attenzione!* at the passers-by and housewives armed with shopping bags mingle happily with the tourists.

### **3 Merceria and church of San Salvador★**

**Church every day 9.30am-5.30pm.**

The Baroque façade of the church of San Salvador conceals many marvels, including some paintings by Titian and the beautiful *Cena in Emaus* by Bellini, which is a copy, but a period one at least. The same succession of shops runs the length of the Mercerie San Salvador. Some are worth stopping at, others less so. Once you have established which ones are the quality shops, and which sell bland 'touristy' items, you are in for a good time.

### **4 Fondaco dei Tedeschi★★**

This is the main post office of Venice. Buying stamps or phoning from within the walls of this venerable *fondaco* (15th-century), which was originally decorated with frescoes by Giorgione and Titian (the ones that could be saved are now at the Ca' d'Oro, see p. 63), is actually quite exciting. Especially when you know that the building was once the headquarters of the German merchants (the *Tedeschi*) who traded with the Serenissima.

### **5 Antica Carbonera restaurant★★**

**Calle Bembo, 4648 ☎ 041 522 54 79 Every day except Thu., Fri. lunchtime and Aug.**

A smiling reception, an elegant but unpretentious setting (it's rather like being on a boat), and some of the best value for money in the vicinity of Piazza San Marco. Choose spaghetti *alle vongole* (with clams)

and a very rare steak washed down with a good Venetian wine, and you can't fail to be content.

### **6 SHOP OF THE CASTER VALESE★★**

**Calle Fiubera, 793 San Marco ☎ 041 522 72 82 Every day except Sun. 10.30am-12.30pm, 3-7pm out of season, 10.30am-7pm in season.**

Since 1918, the name Alberto Valese has been the last word in the art of casting *alla veneziana*. The shop is entirely devoted to bronze, tin, copper and cast-iron and is overflowing with lamps, door knockers and key rings. Here you can buy one of the fifty types of little horses that adorn the sides of gondolas, which are made the traditional way in moulds filled with sand from the Forest of Fontainebleau. The foundry (Fondamenta Madonna dell'Orto, 3535 Cannaregio ☎ 041 72 02 34) can be visited by appointment.

# The Accademia district:
## peace and tranquillity

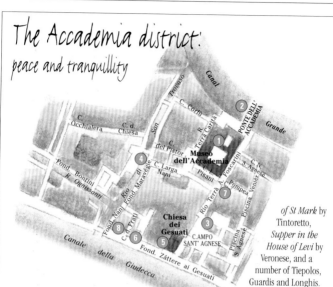

*of St Mark* by Tintoretto, *Supper in the House of Levi* by Veronese, and a number of Tiepolos, Guardis and Longhis.

S ilence reigns along the tranquil *rios*. The occasional steamer passes along the Canale della Giudecca, and the air carries the scent of the sea. Craftsmen still patiently and meticulously construct gondolas with as little regard for the passage of time as the district itself.

## ❶ Museo dell' Accademia★★★
**Every day 9am-7pm, 8pm Sun.**
☎ **041 522 22 47**
**Entry charge.**

Venice's largest museum possesses an amazing number of masterpieces. It's just a pity the lighting's so bad. Avoid late afternoons in winter. Among the paintings you simply must see are *Miracle of the True Cross at San Lorenzo* by Bellini, the *Legend of St Ursula* by Carpaccio, the *Tempesta* by Giorgione, the *Pietà* by Titian, the *Miracle*

## ❷ Ponte dell'Accademia★
This iron bridge was built by the Austrians in 1854, then demolished under Mussolini before being rebuilt in its original form in 1985. It offers a fine view of the Grand Canal and its succession of palaces dominated by the silhouette of the church of Santa Maria della Salute.

### **3** Campo Sant' Agnese★
**Church closed to the public.**

A quiet *campo* that has kept its medieval face intact. For a change, no-one thought it necessary to give the old church of

### **4** RIO AND SQUERO SAN TROVASO★★

**Church every day exc. Sun. 8-11am, 3-6pm**
☎ **041 522 21 33.**

The Palladian church dedicated to St Gervase and St Protase (*Trovaso* is the contraction of Gervasio and Protasio) dominates this charming place. The wooden shacks of the Squero San Trovaso (closed to the public), one of the oldest gondola yards in the city, lie at the junction of two canals. The skiffs that are the very soul of Venice are still made here in accordance with age-old tradition.

Sant'Agnese (12th- to 13th-century) a Baroque makeover. It's the ideal place to stop and dream.

### **5** Church of Gesuati★
**Every day 8am-noon**
☎ **041 523 06 25.**

The façade of the old Jesuit church (18th-century) is the counterpart of the large Palladian buildings on the other side of the Canale della Giudecca (see p. 64). The interior conceals a stunning trompe-l'œil ceiling by Tiepolo (*Apotheosis of St Dominic*).

### **6** Zattere ai Gesuati★

The wide banks of the canal (literally 'pontoons') provide one of the Venetians' favourite places to walk – a popular spot for sunbathing, jogging, eating ice-cream or having a drink.

### **7** Hotel-restaurant Agli Alboretti★
**Rio terrà A. Foscarini, 882-884**
☎ **041 523 00 58**
**Every day except Wed. and Thu. lunchtime, 12.30-2.30pm, 7.30-8.30pm**
**Closed in Jan. and Aug.**

A small family hotel (reservations essential) a

stone's throw from the Accademia. It's quiet and friendly, like the district itself. In the morning you can have breakfast outside in the shady garden, and the excellent restaurant is one of the best in the square.

### **8** Gelateria Nico
**Zattere, 922 Dorsoduro**
☎ **041 522 52 93**
**Every day 8am-10pm**
**Closed end Nov. - Jan.**

This is the home of ice cream, so don't be put off by the formica setting. If you're going to try a delicious *gianduiotto* (whipped ice cream with a stick of chocolate), it's now or never. In summer, you can sun yourself on the terrace overlooking the island of the Giudecca.

# Punta della Dogana: the call of the sea

Punta della Dogana, dominated by the massive triumphal church of Santa Maria della Salute, certainly isn't the best place to go on a spending spree or to mingle with the crowds. People mainly come to this part of the *sestiere* of Dorsoduro (meaning 'hard back' or 'spine') to escape the hustle and bustle and get some fresh air. The peaceful *calle*, little squares and the banks of the Giudecca canal are the perfect location for a romantic stroll.

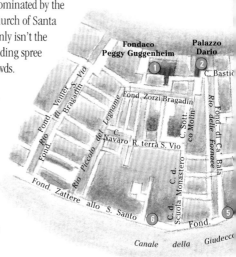

the great artists of the first half of the 20th century, from Picasso and Mondrian to De Chirico and Pollock are present in this unfinished 18th-century palace. As might be expected, the Surrealists feature prominently. Before you leave, visit the pleasant cafeteria or take a look in the museum shop, which is full of gift ideas.

on the perilous role of ambassador of Venice to the Ottoman Empire in the late 15th century.

## ❶ Fondaco Peggy Guggenheim★★★
**Every day except Tue.**
**11am–6pm**
☎ **041 520 62 88**
**Entry charge.**

The woman who was briefly Max Ernst's wife had two consuming passions – her dogs (buried in the garden) and contemporary art. All

## ❷ Palazzo Dario★★

This delightful palace on the Grand Canal, with a façade resembling that of a jewellery box, is more like the work of a sculptor or painter than that of an architect. It used to be the residence of Giovanni Dario, who took

## ❸ Church of San Gregorio★
**Closed to the public.**

People actually work in this beautiful 15th-century church. It's where most of Venice's works of art are sent when they need to be restored. It goes without saying, therefore, that the workshops are always busy.

anal Grande

San Gregorio
Terrà dei tecúmeni

Santa Maria della Salute

C. d. Salute
R. d. Salute
Fond. d. Salute
C. d. Squero

ttere ai Salon

a ai Saloni

### **7** CHURCH OF SANTA MARIA DELLA SALUTE ★★★

**Every day 9am-noon, 3-6.30pm**
☎ 041 522 55 58.

Venice erected this large rotunda in 1630 to thank the Virgin for ending the terrible plague epidemic then raging in the city. The Festival of the Salute (see p. 21) still dutifully commemorates the event. The architect of this masterly example of Baroque art, Baldassare Longhena, didn't skimp on the statues or pinnacle turrets, or on the diameter of the dome either. Once inside, you feel very small, but the overall effect is stunning.

### **5** Zattere ai Saloni and allo Santo Spirito★

**Church Sun. 8am-noon, 3-6pm.**

### **4** Dogana di Mara and Punta della Dogana★★

If you're looking for a pleasant stroll, follow the Punta della Dogana round under the arcades of the old 17th-century Maritime Customs House. It's not difficult to picture the ships that once docked here, and the illustrious artists who fell in love with the place, including Canaletto, Turner and Monet.

Walk along opposite the island of the Giudecca, past the old salt warehouses, the church of Santo Spirito and a number of very tempting terraces. Music lovers shouldn't miss taking a look at the Ospedale degli Incurabili (closed to the public), once reserved for syphilitics, before becoming a boarding school for gifted young musicians.

### **6** Linea d'Ombra restaurant★★
**Punta della Dogana, 19**
☎ 041 520 47 20
**Every day except Wed. and Sun. evening 8pm-2am.**

An elegant restaurant and piano-bar where you can have dinner or a cocktail in the cool of the evening (until 2am) on the banks of the Canale della Giudecca. In summer there's a terrace where you can watch the boats go by.

# The Campo di Santa Margherita district:
## Village Venice

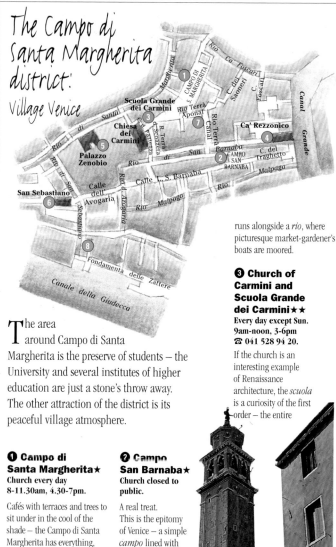

runs alongside a *rio*, where picturesque market-gardener's boats are moored.

### ❸ Church of Carmini and Scuola Grande dei Carmini ★★
**Every day except Sun. 9am-noon, 3-6pm. ☎ 041 528 94 20.**

If the church is an interesting example of Renaissance architecture, the *scuola* is a curiosity of the first order – the entire

The area around Campo di Santa Margherita is the preserve of students – the University and several institutes of higher education are just a stone's throw away. The other attraction of the district is its peaceful village atmosphere.

### ❶ Campo di Santa Margherita ★
**Church every day 8-11.30am, 4.30-7pm.**

Cafés with terraces and trees to sit under in the cool of the shade – the Campo di Santa Margherita has everything, (including concerts and plays in the summer). If you're keen on trompe-l'œil ceilings, be sure not to miss the one in the nearby church of San Pantalon. It's all the more amazing for being a canvas, not a fresco.

### ❼ Campo San Barnaba ★
**Church closed to public.**

A real treat. This is the epitomy of Venice – a simple *campo* lined with a few cafés, dominated as you'd expect by a church flanked by a magnificent 14th-century bell tower. From here a quiet *fondamenta*

### ❹ CA' REZZONICO★★★

**Every day except Fri.**
**10am-4pm**
☎ 041 241 01 00
**Closed until Jan. 2001**
**Entry charge.**

The Venetian palaces can be frustrating. You imagine interiors that are as magnificent, opulent and unique as their exteriors, but their doors are often closed. This venerable building (18th-century), with its sublime interior decoration (marble, trompe-l'œil and painted ceilings), will leave

you speechless with admiration and have you fantasising about the riches hidden inside the city's other palaces. The museum collection is devoted exclusively to Venetian painting of the Enlightenment, and will leave you with a lasting impression if you like the work of Canaletto, Tiepolo and Longhi.

decoration of the upper floor was entrusted to Tiepolo. Yet again, the great Baroque painter shows himself to be an undisputed master of movement.

### ❺ Palazzo Zenobio★★

**Visits by appointment**
☎ 041 522 87 70.

With its Baroque façade, the late 17th-century Palazzo Zenobio may at first seem incongruous under the Venetian sky. The interior is a marvel of trompe-l'œil decoration, a festival of stucco, antique furniture, gilded frames and Venetian mirrors.

### ❻ Church of San Sebastiano★★★

**Every day except Tue.**
**2.30-5.30pm.**

This church, beneath a modest exterior, conceals one of the most dazzling cycles that Veronese ever painted for the Serenissima. Everything, from the ceiling with its trompe-l'œil frescoes to the altarpieces, and

even the organ under which the artist is buried, was executed by Paolo Caliari, otherwise known as Veronese.

### ❼ L'Incontro★

**Campo di S. Margherita, 3062**
☎ 041 522 24 04
**Every day except Tue.**
**lunchtime 12.30-2.30pm,**
**7.30-10.30pm.**

An original restaurant in the Campo di S. Margherita where you can sample a cuisine you

may not have tried before: Sardinian. The terrace is an ideal spot for watching the lively scene in the *campo*.

### ❽ Trattoria San Basilio★

**Fondamenta Zattere, 1516**
☎ 041 521 00 28
**Every day except Sun.**
**noon-3pm, 7-11pm.**

A flawless setting and a quiet terrace – all the ingredients necessary for the proper enjoyment of a refreshing salad and veal's liver prepared the Venetian way.

◀ *Rio di Santa Margherita*

# Around the Rialto: the heart of Venice

The area around the Rialto has rung with the cries of fishmongers and fruit and vegetable sellers for centuries. Even today, nothing has changed, people still converge here each morning to shop in an atmosphere that's truly Mediterranean.

## ❶ Ruga degli Orefici and Ruga Vecchia★

The Street of the Goldsmiths (*Ruga degli Orefici* or *degli Oresi*) and the 'Old Street' (*Ruga Vecchia*) resemble the shopping streets in a village. They're extremely lively when the market's in full swing, between 11am and noon. More jeweller's

shops can be found under the arcades of the gallery parallel to the Ruga degli Orefici.

## ❷ Fabbriche Vecchie and Nuove★
Closed to the public.

The arcaded buildings that once housed the administration of trade, and of navigation and supplies, have stood beside the Grand Canal since the 16th century. Built

respectively by Scarpagnino and Sansovino, they today house the court of justice.

## ❸ Pescheria★
**Market Tue.-Sat.**
**8am-noon.**

This is Venice's fish market, where Venetian housewives come to shop after their

obligatory trip to the Erberia fruit and vegetable market (every day except Sun. 8am-noon).

## ❹ Church and campo of San Cassiano★
**Church every day except Sun.**
**8am-noon, 4.30-7pm**
☎ **041 72 14 08.**

The church itself is a patchwork of styles housing an unusual *Crucifixion* by Tintoretto. But the real charm of the place lies elsewhere, in the quiet *campo* bordered by the Rio Cassiano.

## ❺ Ca' Pesaro★★
**Museum of Modern Art**
☎ **041 72 11 27**
**Museum of Oriental Art**
☎ **041 524 11 73**
**Every day except Mon.**
**9am-2pm**
**(separate entry tickets).**

Designed by Longhena in the late 17th century, this palace houses works that were bought at the first Venice Biennales. The ground floor, devoted to

19th-century Italian painting, may not be particularly exciting, but the first floor houses some real treasures including a very fine Klimt. Whatever happens, don't miss the collection of Japanese art in the Oriental museum.

## ❻ Trattoria Poste Vecie★
**Campo della Pescaria, 1608**
☎ **041 72 18 22**
**Every day except Tue.**
**noon-3pm, 7.30-11pm.**

This trattoria near the fish market, a stone's throw from the Grand Canal, is

## ❼ PONTE DI RIALTO★★

Without the Rialto Bridge, the main link beween the two banks of Venice's Grand Canal, it wouldn't be the city it is today. Built of stone in the late 16th century, the 'Rialto' remained the only bridge over the Grand Canal until the 19th century. It was difficult to build and progress was slow. Not only did it rest on unstable ground, but its height was considered an amazing feat for the time (7.5m/25ft, to allow the galleys to pass underneath). As in Florence, gold and silversmiths set up shop on it, and several of the portico shops still carry on the tradition.

said to be the oldest in Venice. Whether this is true or not, the *insalata di cape sante* (scallop salad) is excellent, as are the other fish dishes. There's a fine wine list, too.

## ❽ Osteria Do Mori★
**Calle dei Do Mori, 429**
☎ **041 522 54 01**
**Every day except Sun.**
**9am-9pm.**

An old, typically Venetian *osteria* where you can taste all sorts of Venetian wines as you sample the local dishes such as ox tongue. You can also have a sandwich standing at the old counter, but there isn't always a great deal of space.

# The Frari district:
## the treasures of the churches and scuole

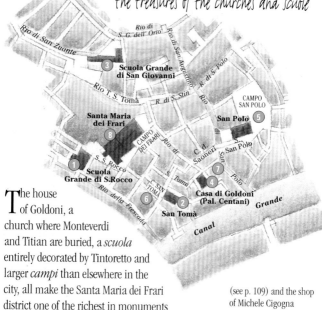

The house of Goldoni, a church where Monteverdi and Titian are buried, a *scuola* entirely decorated by Tintoretto and larger *campi* than elsewhere in the city, all make the Santa Maria dei Frari district one of the richest in monuments in the Serenissima.

### ❶ Scuola Grande di San Rocco★★★
*Scuola* every day
Apr.-Nov., 9am-5.30pm,
Dec.-Mar. 10am-4pm
☎ 041 523 48 64
Entry charge.
Church Mon.-Fri. 7.30am-
12.30pm, Sat.-Sun.
7.30am-12.30pm, 2-4pm
☎ 041 523 48 64.

Imagine two floors entirely covered in paintings by Tintoretto and you'll have some idea of how marvellous this is – it's an absolute must. Fans of Jacopo Robusti can't afford to miss the Renaissance church opposite.

### ❷ Church and campo of San Tomà★★
Church closed to the public.

A small square dominated by an 18th-century church. Opposite is the former *scuola* of the shoemakers, the portal of which is adorned with an interesting bas-relief. There are many well-heeled visitors to the square, since two of the big names in Venetian fashion reside here: the jeweller Sfriso

(see p. 109) and the shop of Michele Cigogna (see p. 57).

### ❸ Scuola Grande di San Giovanni★★
Visits by appointment
☎ 041 523 39 97.

Worth seeing just for the magnificent marble portal by Pietro Lombardo (c.1480) embossed with an eagle, the symbol of John the Baptist.

### ❹ Casa di Goldoni★
Closed for restoration
☎ 041 523 63 53.

The house where the playwright Goldoni was born opens onto a narrow *calle*, along which you can enter the pretty interior courtyard.

### ❺ Campo and church of San Polo★

Church every day 7.30am-noon, 4-7pm, Sun. 8am-noon
☎ 041 523 76 31
Entry charge (*Stations of the Cross* by Tiepolo only).

The *campo* sometimes seems a little empty, but it livens up for the Carnival and for the *Mostra* (open-air films). If you're thirsty, there are a few cafés here, as well as a fountain that works, which is rare in Venice. The sober church houses a series of small paintings by Tiepolo.

### ❻ Shop of Michele Cigogna★★

Campo San Tomà, 2867
☎ and ☎ 041 522 76 78
Every day except Sun.
9am-12.30pm, 3-6.30pm.

A well-established restorer and manufacturer of traditional furniture and paintings, with a workshop dating from the 19th century. The little painted wooden caskets in the shop window are tempting but pricey, as are the gilded frames. Michele Cigogna also paints pictures to order.

### ❼ Osteria Alla Patatina★★

Ponte San Polo, 2742
☎ 041 523 72 38
Every day except Sun.
9.30am-2.30pm,
4.30-9pm.

The Osteria Alla Patatina is just the place to tuck into *polpette* (meatballs), vegetables and chips. What a pity they stop serving as early as 9pm!

### ❽ CHURCH OF SANTA MARIA DEI FRARI★★★

Every day except Sun.
9am-5pm
☎ 041 522 26 37
Entry charge.

Grandiose, imposing, massive, moving – words cannot adequately describe this early 15th-century church. It is a fine example of Venetian Gothic architecture at its peak. The dazzling interior houses an amazing collection of works of art that are among the best that Venice has produced. It's difficult to know which way to look first – at the brilliant *Assumption* by Titian (on the high altar), which has been called the most beautiful painting in the world, the mellow Bellini (in the sacristy) or the strange pyramidal tomb by Canova.

# Riva degli Schiavoni:
## a walk alla veneziana

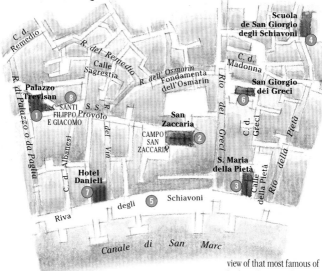

The large luxury hotels on the Riva degli Schiavoni have one of the finest views in the world. Only a handful of tourists bother to go on any further, and a good thing too. Peace and quiet are vital to appreciate the important sights concealed behind the village atmosphere of this part of the *sestiere* of Castello.

### ❶ Rio di Palazzo o da Paglia★★

From the Ponte della Paglia, on the *rio* of the same name, you can get the best possible view of that most famous of bridges, the Ponte dei Sospiri (Bridge of Sighs, 17th-century). The bridge linked the prisons to the court of the Doge's palace, and the defendants would sigh as they crossed it, hence its name.

### ❷ Church of San Zaccaria★★

Every day 10am–noon, 4–6pm
☎ 041 522 12 57
Entry charge for chapel.

The interior of this Renaissance church is every bit as charming as the exterior. It contains one of the finest, if not the finest work by Giovanni Bellini – a Virgin and Child, naturally.

In a side chapel (entry charge), 15th-century altarpieces drip with gold, and there are frescoes by the Florentine Castagno.

### ❸ Church of Santa Maria della Pietà★
**Closed except for concerts**
☎ 041 523 10 96.

Vivaldi, who was the *maestro di cappella* of the Ospedale della Pietà until 1740, wasn't acquainted with the present

church, which was rebuilt shortly after his death. Yet the oval room, from which all sharp angles have been banished for acoustic reasons, rings today with the *concerti* of the 'red priest' (so called because of the colour of his hair). If there's a concert on, then do go.

### ❹ Scuola di San Giorgio degli Schiavoni★★★
**Every day except Mon.**
**10am-12.30pm**
**(and 3-6pm in season)**
☎ 041 522 88 28
**Entry charge.**

Although it contains only ten or so paintings by Carpaccio (including a beautiful St George slaying the dragon), it is one of the major sights of Venice and an absolute must. Nothing has changed here since the 16th century.

### ❺ Riva degli Schiavoni★★
The Serenissima has dedicated one of its most

beautiful quays to the Slavs (Schiavoni) of Dalmatia. Forget about the *vaporetti* and ignore the (rare) traces of modernity and you'll think you've stepped into a painting by Canaletto or de Guardi.

### ❻ Church of San Giorgio dei Greci and icon museum★★
**Mon.-Sat. 9am-12.30pm, 2-4.30pm,**
**Sun. 10am-5pm**
☎ 041 522 65 81
**Entry charge for museum.**

Come to the Orthodox Mass here to breathe in the heady incense and hark back to a time when the Serenissima had a special relationship with Constantinople. In addition, visit the *scuola*, with its rich collection of icons executed by Byzantine artists in Venice after their flight from the Ottoman Empire. You'll be lost in wonder as you stroll through the timeless museum, a large room with a polished wooden floor that creaks satisfyingly underfoot.

### ❼ Hotel Danieli ★★
**Riva degli Schiavoni, 4196**
☎ 041 522 64 80
**⒡ 041 520 02 08.**

This dream of a place, with its chandeliers, antique furniture and thick carpets isn't cheap, but at least you'll be able to say you've walked in the footsteps of the great, from Balzac and de Musset to George Sand and Wagner.

### ❽ Da Aciugheta restaurant★
**Campiello Santi Filippo e Giacomo, 4357**
☎ 041 522 42 92
**Every day except Wed. in winter, 11.30am-3pm, 7.30-11pm.**

It isn't always easy to find a good restaurant in this district, but here's one that's really excellent. Try the speciality – *pizzette* (small pizzas) with *aciugheta* (anchovies).

# The Santa Maria Formosa and San Giovanni e Paolo district

The *campi* of this district are home to the fruit and vegetable sellers and florists, while the shops beside the narrow *calle* quickly fill up with people at lunchtime. The maze of streets contains such a wealth of curiosities that it's difficult to see them all. Do try to come back at night, though, when only cats are left wandering the alleyways.

**❶ Church and campo of Santa Maria Formosa★★**
Mon.-Sat. 10am-5pm, Sun. 3-4pm
☎ 041 523 46 45
Entry charge.

This pretty 16th-century church is quite unusual, with its double entrance on a vast *campo* lined with café terraces. The interior, which is very light, houses a *Madonna della Misericordia* (right aisle) by Vivarini that you could never tire of seeing. Close by, the Calle Lunga S. M. Formosa and Calle delle Bande are packed with interesting shops, especially the maskmakers'.

## ❷ Palazzo Querini-Stampalia★★

**Every day except Mon.**
**10am-1pm, 3-6pm**
☎ **041 520 34 33**
**Entry charge.**

This 16th-century palazzo stands on an amusing convoluted *campiello* that's

a mixture of bridges and canals. The foundation's collection allows you to become better acquainted with the art of Bellini, Tiepolo and Longhi. But make sure the museum is open, or you'll be paying to visit the ground floor, which is of little interest.

## ❸ Scuola San Marco★★

**Chapel every day 9am-noon.**

Now the hospital of Venice, the Scuola San Marco has a magnificent asymmetrical façade by Pietro Lombardo decorated with trompe-l'œil motifs and marble panels. The chapel holds works by Tintoretto and Veronese.

## ❹ Statue of the condottiere Bartholomeo Colleoni★★★

The great military leader Colleoni bequeathed his immense fortune to the city on the express condition that his equestrian statue be placed in front of San Marco. Reluctant to infringe an old regulation prohibiting building in front of the basilica, the authorities set up Verrocchio's masterly

work in front of the Scuola San Marco – and pocketed the cash.

## ❺ Church of Santa Maria dei Miracoli★★

**Closed for restoration.**

A real gem. The exterior of this little Renaissance church closely resembles a jewellery box, with its colourful marble panels and beautiful

encrustations. The whole of the surrounding district is also worth a closer look.

## ❻ Antiche Cantine Ardenghi restaurant★

**Calle della Testa, 6369**
**Cannaregio**
☎ **041 523 76 91**
**Every day exc. Sun.**
**10am-11pm.**

A nice, inexpensive *osteria* whose walls are decorated with photographs. You can sample a number of traditional Venetian dishes

## ❼ CHURCH OF SAN GIOVANNI E PAOLO★★★

**Every day 7.30am-**
**12.30pm, 3.30-7pm**
☎ **041 523 75 10.**

Always on the lookout for ways of celebrating itself, the Serenissima spared no expense when building and embellishing San Zanipolo (a contraction of the names Giovanni and Paolo). The 13th- to 15th-century church, which was the pantheon of the Doges, is quite breathtaking. No fewer than twenty-five of the powerful men who built Venice lie here side by side. In this sculpture museum, don't miss the tombs of the Doges Mocenigo (right aisle), Vendramin (choir) and Marcelo (left aisle), all of which are by Pietro Lombardo. The interior of the church also houses a staggering quantity of paintings by Bellini, Veronese and Piazzetta.

here, such as pasta and bean soup (*pasta e fagiuoli*), rice soup with peas (*risi e bisi*) and delicious San Daniele and other hams.

# The Ghetto and Madonna dell'Orto district: Venice unmasked

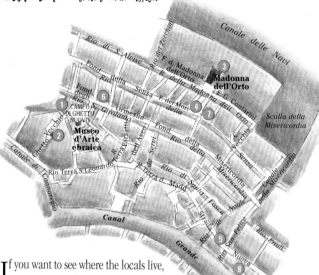

If you want to see where the locals live, Cannaregio, with its quiet *fondamente* (quays), canals and broad, airy streets is definitely the place to visit. As you stroll along or open the doors of the *osterie*, you'll come face to face with the true population of Venice.

## ❶ Ghetto Nuovo and Museo d'Arte Ebraica★★

Museum every day except Sat. 10am-4pm (7pm Jun.-Sep.)
☎ 041 71 53 59
3 synagogues: guided tour (enquire at museum) every day 10.30am-3.30pm (5.30pm Jun.-Sep.)
Entry charge.

Entirely surrounded by canals, the Ghetto Nuovo is a vast esplanade surrounded by 'skyscrapers'

(buildings over 5 storeys high). There are still a few Jewish businesses here (a kosher restaurant and a craft shop), Ashkenazy synagogues and a museum of Jewish art with gold and silver plate and superb fabrics dating from the 17th and 18th centuries.

## ❷ Ghetto Vecchio★★

Despite their size, the houses of the Ghetto Vecchio were unable to accommodate the Jewish community after 1540. It therefore spread to the quiet district of the old foundry (*geto*), around the magnificent Spanish synagogue (Scuola Spagnola), with its polished wood interior.

## ❸ Church of Madonna dell'Orto★★

**Every day 10am-5.30pm**
☎ **041 71 99 33.**

Fans of Tintoretto shouldn't miss this 15th-century church for anything. Behind a red and white façade, the tomb of the painter and a large number of his works are housed.

## ❹ Campo dei Mori★

This quiet, soulful *campo* owes its name to the strange statues of Moors built into the houses. Don't miss the bas-relief of the Palazzo Mastelli opposite the house

## ❽ CA' D'ORO★★★

**Every day 9am-2pm**
☎ **041 523 87 90.**

If we could keep only one of the countless palaces strung out along the Grand Canal, it would be this one. The Ca' d'Oro (15th-century), which takes its name from the gold adorning its elegant façade, is the most profoundly Venetian, in other words it is the most refined, of all the palaces with an interior to match. If you like the bronzes and paintings of the Renaissance see the sublime *St Sebastian* by Andrea Mantegna in its splendid frame. You're sure to find this one of the three most interesting museums in the city. From the loggia you'll have a superb view of the Rialto and its busy market into the bargain.

of Tintoretto (no. 3,398) on the *fondamenta*. It serves to remind us that this was once the Arab merchant district.

## ❺ Strada Nuova★

Built in the 19th century, the Strada Nuova is the main shopping street in Venice and a good place to buy pastries, wine and other knick-knacks. Tucked away in the little streets on either side, there are typical old *osterie* (inns).

## ❻ Barada restaurant★

**Fondamenta Ormesini, 2754**
☎ **041 71 59 77**
**Every day except Sun.**
**6pm-2am.**

A pleasant terrace beside a *fondamenta* where you can sample excellent Syrian-Libyan dishes washed down with *raki*. It's a good place to come if you're tired of spaghetti *al nero di seppia* (in cuttlefish ink) or veal's liver done the Venetian way.

## ❼ Cantina ai Mori wine merchants★

**Fondamenta ai Mori, 3386 Cannaregio**
**Every day except Sun. 9am-1pm, 4.30-7pm.**

*Il signore* Baffo, a wine merchant by trade, claims that his family has been Venetian for generations. He's descended from an illustrious family, one of whose members, Safiyé, married the Ottoman sultan Murat III. The shop is full of barrels, which are home to the very best wines of Venetia.

# The islands of the Giudecca and San Giorgio Maggiore

*[map of the Giudecca island showing:]*
Canale del Laurranti
Fond. San Biagio
① Mulino Stucky
⑥ Fond. S. Eufemia
Fond. Ponte Piccolo
Fond. di
Canale della Giudecc...
R. de Ponte Longo
Fond. S. Giacomo
GIUDECCA
② Chiesa del Redentore

The island of the Giudecca, originally the place to which Venetian families that had been tried and found guilty (*giudicato*) were exiled, and later, in the 16th century, the home of patricians in search of some greenery, is now a charming, if underpopulated, working-class suburb.

### ❶ Mulino Stucky★
**Closed for restoration.**

This enormous, red neo-Gothic flour mill adds a curiously modern, industrial touch to the island of the Giudecca. It bears the name of its former owner, the Swiss Stucky, who was murdered by one of his employees in 1910.

### ❷ Church of Redentore★★
**Every day 8am-noon, 4-7pm**
☎ 041 523 14 15.

This pure collection of geometrical shapes was built by Palladio following the end of the plague of 1576 that wiped out a third of the population of Venice. Every year on the Festa del Rendentore (see p. 21), a bridge made out of boats is set up over the Canale della Giudecca from the Zattere opposite.

### ❸ Convent of Zitelle★
**Convent closed to the public.**

Designed by Palladio and crowned with the obligatory dome, the church owes its name to the old maids (*zitelle*) of the adjacent convent, who were said to be skilled lacemakers. Behind the church, on the south side of the island,

is one of Venice's most notable hotels, the Cipriani (see p. 75), with its fabulous terrace opening onto the lagoon.

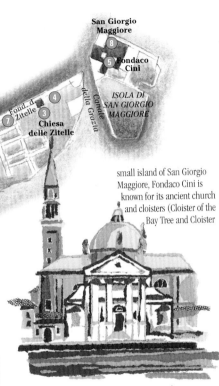

**San Giorgio Maggiore**

**8**

**5** **Fondaco Cini**

*ISOLA DI SAN GIORGIO MAGGIORE*

Canale della Grazia

**4**

Fond. d Zitelle

**7** **3**

**Chiesa delle Zitelle**

## **8** CHURCH OF SAN GIORGIO MAGGIORE★★★

**Every day 9.30am-12.30pm, 2.30-5.30pm (7pm in summer)**
**☎ 041 528 99 00**
**Entry charge (lift) for bell tower.**

This church is a lesson in architecture. Once again, and even more so than before, Palladio will delight you with his admiration for the forms of Ancient Rome. It's difficult not to be moved in the face of such conviction, although the interior, which houses important works by Tintoretto (choir and sacristy), is somewhat overpowering and a little bit cold as well. Make a beeline for the top of the bell tower. There, in the company of a monk, you'll have an absolutely fabulous view of the lagoon, which is even finer than the one from the campanile of Piazza San Marco.

small island of San Giorgio Maggiore, Fondaco Cini is known for its ancient church and cloisters (Cloister of the Bay Tree and Cloister

## **4** Tre Oci★
**Closed to the public.**
This strange neo-Gothic palace, which was built by a painter in the early 20th century, owes its name to the three curious windows that look out over the Canale della Giudecca.

## **5** Fondaco Cini★★
**Closed except for cultural events.**
Occupying a large part of the

of the Cypresses).
If, by any chance, there's an exhibition, play or concert on while you're in Venice, make sure you go.

## **6** Harry's Dolci restaurant★★
**Fondamenta San Biagio, 773**
**☎ 041 522 48 44**
**Every day except Tue. and Nov.-Mar.**
**10.30am-3pm, 7-10.30pm.**
The off-shoot of Harry's Bar (see p. 76) is very pleasant when the sun is shining, and the bill will turn out to be slightly less ruinous in comparison.
This is the place to sample a Bellini or a delicious pastry in

the company of Venetian polite society.

## **7** Bar-restaurant Iguana★
**Fondamenta della Misericordia, 2515**
**☎ 041 71 35 61**
**Every day except Mon.**
**8am-3pm, 6pm-1am.**
Venice is gradually getting into the swing of things and now has a tex-mex restaurant. It's a good, inexpensive place to have a bite to eat in the sun while taking in the view from the Giudecca.

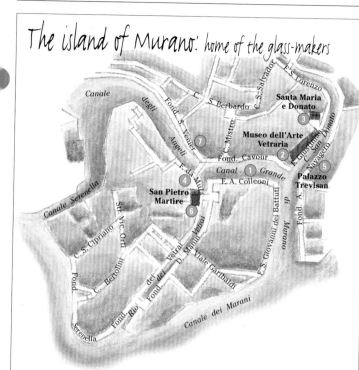

*The island of Murano: home of the glass-makers*

Canale

Canale

C. S. Berbardo

Fond. S. Venier degli Angeli

C.-S.-Salvador

F. S. Lorenzo

**Santa Maria e Donato** ③

C. Mistro

**Museo dell'Arte Vetraria** ②

Fond. Cavour

F. da Mula

Canal ① Grande

F. A. Colleoni

F. Giustinian

C. San Donato

Navagero

⑦

④

**San Pietro Martire**

⑥

**Palazzo Trevisan** ⑤

Fond. A.

F. S. Giovanni dei Battiuti

di Murano

Canale Serenella

Sfr. Vic. Orti

C. S. Cipriano

C. Benolini

Fond.

dei Vetrai

D. Manin Vetrai

Viale Garibaldi

Fond. Rio

Fond.

Serenella

Canale dei Marani

With its canal, which is large only in name, its comparably modest palaces and fewer churches, Murano is like a miniature version of Venice. Everything here revolves around the glass manufacturing industry of which it's so proud.

### ❶ Canal Grande★★

The Canal Grande winds its way gracefully through the string of islands that make up Murano. As in Venice, the nobles built palaces on the banks. These were originally surrounded by gardens where the nobles would sit in summer to keep cool. The glass factories are more modest in appearance: these housed the living quarters, warehouse and workshop used by the master glass-maker and his apprentices.

### ❷ Museo dell'Arte Vetraria or Museo Vetrario★★

**Every day except Wed. 10am-4pm, 5pm in summer**
☎ **041 73 95 86**
**Entry charge.**

The Palazzo Giustinian (17th-century) is so interesting that you'll soon forget the less than lively presentation. Besides gaining an insight into the development of Murano glass

and the various techniques used in its manufacture, you can see the creations of the greatest masters of the art, beginning with Angelo Barrovier (1405–1460). After admiring all these treasures, you'll undoubtedly view the island's shop windows with a new perspective and avoid any rash decisions to purchase a souvenir made in Hong Kong. Before leaving, take a closer look at the fine façade.

### ❸ Church of Santa Maria e Donato★★★
**Every day. 8am-noon, 4-7pm.**

You can't help wondering why this 12th-century church has its back to the

canal, but the reason is in fact simple – the apse looks fantastic reflected in the water. The interior isn't bad, either. Besides the mosaic on a gold background in the apse, the church has incredible paving that's as dazzling, if not more so, than that of San Marco, which is no small praise.

### ❹ MAZZEGA★
**Ponte Vivarini, 3 and fondamenta da Mula, 147, Murano**
☎ **041 73 68 88**
🖷 **041 73 90 79**
**Every day except Sun. (in winter only) 9am-5pm.**

Opposite the Ponte Vivarini, a showroom of one of the great names of Murano glass displays a stunning collection of its finest past and present creations. The vases, services, chandeliers and antique jewellery on display make an incredible sight. If you think (quite rightly)

that all this could make a considerable dent in your bank account, think of it as an investment and you won't regret it. The workshop is just next door and is open to visitors.

### ❺ Palazzo Trevisan★
**Closed for restoration.**

This palace, attributed to Palladio, is the finest on the island and definitely the equal of the Palazzo Giustinian opposite.

### ❻ Church of San Pietro Martire★
**Every day 8am-noon, 4-7pm**
☎ **041 73 97 04.**

Althought the exterior of this church is not exactly

memorable, it's worth paying a visit to see its many works of art, some of which are lit by chandeliers (Murano glass, of course). These include a Madonna by Bellini, canvases by Veronese and Tintoretto and many other wonders.

### ❼ Trattoria Ai Frati★
**Fondamenta Venier, 4**
☎ **041 73 66 94**
**Every day except Thu. noon-3pm**
**Closed for 3 weeks after the Carnival.**

A tourist restaurant serving good traditional Venetian cuisine. Sit on the terrace and order an *anguilla sull'ara* (baked eel) – it's quite delicious.

# The islands of Burano and Torcello:
## fishermen and lacemakers

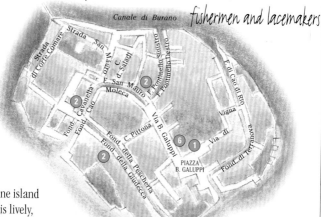

Canale di Burano

One island is lively, while the other is delightfully nostalgic. Burano's multicoloured houses and numerous lace shops line the banks of the small canals. Torcello, which was the capital of the lagoon until the 10th century, now has only a handful of inhabitants. Wild and isolated, the island would in fact be completely deserted if its ancient cathedral wasn't there to attract and delight visitors.

## ❶ Scuola dei merletti di Burano★★

**Every day except Tue.**
**10am-4pm**
☎ **041 73 00 34**
**Entry charge.**

You really should visit Burano's lace (*merletti*) museum first before rushing into buying anything. Pay special attention to the finishing pieces of the school of lacemakers. Each of them took several months to make and is comparable to the work of a goldsmith. If you then go and look at all the lace place mats,

blouses and so forth on sale in the Via Galuppi they're sure to suffer by comparison.

## ❷ The *Fondamente* and the houses of Burano★★

Fishermen used to paint their houses in bright colours so that they could spot them from a distance. The most attractive groups of these simple dwellings aren't to be found in the most crowded place – along the street dedicated to the local celebrity, the musician Baldassare Galuppi (1706–1785), known as Il Buranello – but rather by the side of simple *fondamente* (such as the Fondamenta della Giudecca) or little *calle*.

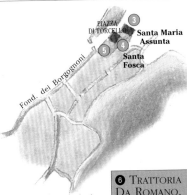

## ❸ Cathedral of Santa Maria Assunta★★★
**Every day**
**10am-12.30pm, 2-5pm**
☎ 041 73 00 84.

Ernest Hemingway was enchanted by this old cathedral (11th-century). With its elegant bell tower rising from the long grass, it's not difficult to see why. Its mosaics (12th- and 13th- century) are some of the most important examples of Byzantine art; the *Last Judgement* (wall 0), portrays with sadistic pleasure the torments of the damned and would have appealed to Bosch and Brueghel. Also of note are the elegant marble pulpit and the iconostasis (separating the chancel from the nave), the latter decorated with symbolic animals.

## ❹ Church of Santa Fosca★
**Every day**
**10am-noon, 2-6.30pm**
☎ 041 73 00 84.

Squat and round (though octagonal on the inside), the church of Santa Fosca is entered via a magnificent portico. Its architecture harks back to the dawn of Christianity, yet it's a contemporary of its larger neighbour.

## ❺ Hotel-restaurant Locanda Cipriani, Torcello★★
**Isola di Torcello**
☎ 041 73 01 50
**Restaurant open every day except Tue. and Nov.-mid-Mar. noon-3pm.**

One of the lagoon's major restaurants. You can have lunch in the rustic dining-room or under the wide veranda. The house dishes include pasta stuffed with meat, *risotti*, fish and seafood. There are also six rooms so you can spend a peaceful night on the island.

## ❻ TRATTORIA DA ROMANO, BURANO★★
**Via Baldassare Galuppi, 221**
☎ 041 73 00 30
**Every day exc. Tue.**
**and 15 Dec.-15 Feb.**
**noon-3pm, 6.30-10pm.**

One of the best restaurants in the lagoon and also one of the most famous, thanks to the exceptional talent of its hand-picked chefs. Here you'll find an incomparable choice of fish (eel, dory, monkfish, sole and sardines) – each cooked with remarkable skill in a variety of ways (grilled, poached, etc.) – as well as soup, *risotto* and fried dishes. Booking is essential in summer and at the weekend because of tour groups.

*Church of Santa Fosca*

# Rooms and restaurants Practicalities

## HOTEL CATEGORIES AND RATES

There are 6 categories of hotel in Venice, ranging from one star (often called *pensione*) to five stars. They're all expensive. For basic facilities (en-suite shower and toilet), expect to pay around L180,000. For a more comfortable room (with bath, direct phone, television and pleasant surroundings) and hotel service, you have to pay at least L250,000.

These prices are for a double room in high season. Low-season rates apply from December to late January only. They can allow you to make savings of up to 50%.

## RESERVING FROM HOME

The best way to do this is through a tour operator, though you can reserve direct if you go about it early enough (around 2 months in advance in general and up to 6 months if your stay coincides with the Carnival). Phone or fax the hotel to

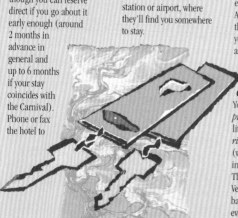

find out what to do. It generally involves sending an international money order (from a Post Office), a fax with your credit card number or a Eurocheque covering the cost of one night's stay.

## ARRIVING WITHOUT A RESERVATION

Don't wander around the city. Go straight to the tourist information office at the station or airport, where they'll find you somewhere to stay.

## CHOOSING A DISTRICT

The hotels near Piazza S. Marco are mainly luxury establishments (3-5 stars). On the other hand, the poetical out-of-the-way districts, especially Dorsoduro, are full of quiet, often charming, little hotels that are less expensive in general than their equivalents in the city centre. As Venice isn't very spread out, they're your best bet if you don't want to stay in a luxury hotel.

## RISTORANTE, TRATTORIA OR OSTERIA

You can still have pizzas in a *pizzeria*, but there's now very little difference between a *ristorante* and a *trattoria* (which used to be more informal and less expensive). The *osteria* or *bacaro* is the Venetian equivalent of a wine bar. Some close early in the evening (around 10pm or even earlier). Most places have a few seats, but the Venetians mainly come here for a quick bite of *cicheti* (a variety of little snacks) and an *ombra* (a glass of wine) standing at the bar. The atmosphere is sometimes fantastic. You can also have a *tramezzino* (triangular sandwich) and a beer in a *birreria* or a hot meal in a *rosticceria* (steakhouse).

## WHERE TO HAVE DINNER

The nearer a restaurant is to Piazza S. Marco, the more expensive it's likely to be. It's better to head for the outlying districts, where the cuisine is better, price for price. The set meals for tourists are tasteless and best avoided. Most eating places are shut on Sundays.

## MEALTIMES

Lunchtime is from noon/1pm to 3pm and dinnertime from 8pm to 9.30pm. It's a good idea to book, especially at well-known places. Otherwise, arrive before the rush, at around 7/7.30pm.

## MEALS AND PRICES

A complete meal consists of 5 courses: the *antipasti* or starter (ham, soup, etc.), the *primo* (pasta) and the *secondo piatto* (meat or fish), the *contorni* (salad or vegetables served

---

### A VENETIAN MEAL

Starter: *carpaccio* (fine slices of beef marinated in oil).
*Primo piatto*: *spaghetti alle vongole* (with clams) or *alle seppie* (with cuttlefish ink).
*Secondo piatto*: *sarde in saor* (sardines marinated with onions, vinegar and pine nuts, then grilled), *baccalà mantecà* (cod beaten with oil, garlic and parsley) or *fegato alla veneziana* (veal's liver on a bed of onions).
*Contorno*: *polenta* (corn bread).
Dessert: *tiramisù* (see p 31).

---

separately) and the *dolci* (desserts). Unless you have a huge appetite, three courses are quite sufficient.

The cost per person, including a carafe of wine, is around L35,000 in an *osteria* and around L150,000 in a smart restaurant. These prices include the *coperto* (cover charge + bread), service (10 %) and a tip or *mancia* (5 % or more).

# HOTELS

## Sestiere of San Marco

### Gritti Palace★★★★★

(see p. 41)

### Cavalletto e Doge Orseolo★★★★

Calle Cavalletto, 1107 (*vaporetti* 1 and 82, S. Marco)
☎ 041 520 09 55
☎ 041 523 81 84.

A small luxury hotel standing in the delightful Bacino Orseolo, a stone's throw from Piazza S. Marco. You'll be lulled by the serenades of the gondoliers just below. It's the ideal place to spend your honeymoon.

### Concordia★★★★

Calle Larga di S. Marco, 367 (*vaporetti* 1 and 82, S. Marco)
☎ 041 520 68 66
☎ 041 520 67 75.

If you must have a view of the Piazza S. Marco (there is a partial view of the basilica from the breakfast room), then this is the hotel for you. Unfortunately, the rooms are a little lacking in character.

### Europa e Regina★★★★

Via Larga XXII Marzo, 2159 (*vaporetti* 1 and 82, S. Marco)
☎ 041 520 04 77
☎ 041 523 15 33.

A sumptuous palace with a fine terrace and a pleasant restaurant on the Grand Canal, where you can dine with a view of the church of S. Maria della Salute.

### Luna★★★★

Calle dell'Ascensione, 1243 (*vaporetti* 1 and 82, S. Marco)
☎ 041 528 98 40
☎ 041 528 71 60.

A wonderful hotel occupying the former seat of the Templars. It has a lounge with 18th-century frescoes and impeccable rooms with a view of the church of S. Giorgio Maggiore.

### Monaco e Grand Canal★★★★

Calle Vallaresso, 1325 (*vaporetti* 1 and 82, S. Marco)
☎ 041 520 02 11
☎ 041 520 05 01.

An elegant, luxury hotel with a façade on the Grand Canal overlooking the churches of S.

Maria della Salute and S. Giorgio Maggiore. Impeccable service and few groups.

### Ala★★★

Campo S. M. del Giglio, 2494 S. Marco (*vaporetto* 1, S. Maria del Giglio)
☎ 041 520 83 33

Midway between Piazza S. Marco and the Accademia, a quiet hotel with simple, comfortable rooms overlooking a pleasant *campo* where the gondoliers meet. Some of the rooms have traditional furniture.

### Bonvecchiati ★★★

Calle Goldoni, 4488 (*vaporetti* 1 and 82, Rialto)
☎ 041 528 50 17
☎ 041 528 52 30.

A charming hotel near Campo S. Tomà that's a little expensive for its category. It has a sumptuous glass canopy and there are modern paintings throughout.

### Flora★★★

Calle Larga XXII Marzo, 2283/A (*vaporetto* 1, S. M. del Giglio)
☎ 041 520 58 44
☎ 041 522 82 17.

Pleasant and well-situated (a few minutes from Piazza S. Marco), with a rather old-fashioned decor. The Liberty

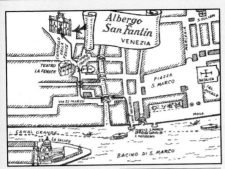

staircase gives access to small rooms overlooking a quiet interior courtyard.

## La Fenice et des Artistes★★★

**Campiello Fenice, 1936 (*vaporetto* 1, S. M. del Giglio)**
☎ 041 523 23 33
📠 041 520 37 21.

A charming *campiello* close to La Fenice theatre is home to one of the nicest hotels in the S. Marco district. It's quiet and shady and you can have breakfast in a little courtyard garden. A first-rate hotel.

### Sestiere of Castello

## Danieli
★★★★★
(see p. 59).

## La Residenza★★

**Campo Bandiera e Moro, 3608 (*vaporetti* 1, 14, 52 and 82, S. Zaccaria)**
☎ 041 528 53 15
📠 041 523 88 59
closed beg. Nov.-beg. Dec. and 6 Jan.-15 Feb.

A superb 15th-century palace with its original decor intact (frescoes in the lounges), in a *campo* far from the crowds. A hotel offering some of the best value for money in Venice.

## Kette★★★

**Piscina S. Moisè, 2053 (*vaporetti* 1 and 82, S. Marco)**
☎ 041 520 77 66
📠 041 522 89 64.

A pleasant place to stay on a quiet *calle* and *rio* not far from La Fenice theatre. Cosy, comfortable rooms.

## San Giorgio★★

**Rio terrà della Mandola, 3781 (*vaporetto* 1, S. Angelo)**
☎ 041 523 58 35
📠 041 522 80 72.

A tastefully decorated hotel without any airs where you'll be welcomed with a smile. Well-located in the most authentic part of the *sestiere* of S. Marco (near Palazzo Fortuny).

## San Fantin★★

**Campiello Fenice, 1930/A (*vaporetti* 1 and 82, S. Marco)**
☎ 041 523 14 01.

A charming little hotel with an original façade decorated with cannon balls celebrating the revolution of 1848. Its well-kept rooms are far more affordable than those of La Fenice et des Artistes next door.

## San Moisè★★★

**Piscina S. Moisè, 2058 (*vaporetti* 1 and 82, S. Marco)**
☎ 041 520 37 55
📠 041 521 06 70.

This well-run establishment in the quiet Fenice district offers

spacious, personalised rooms furnished in a traditional style.

*The sumptuous interior of the Hotel Danieli*

## Sestiere of Dorsoduro

### Accademia Villa Maravege★★★

Fondamenta Bollani, 1058 (*vaporetti* 1 and 82, Accademia)
☎ 041 521 01 88
🖷 041 523 91 52.

This 17th-century residence with a flower-filled courtyard on one side and a garden on the other, is one of the most delightful hotels in Venice. Book several months in advance and avoid the annexe, which is very noisy.

### American★★★

S. Vio, 628 (*vaporetti* 1 and 82, Accademia)
☎ 041 520 47 33
🖷 041 520 40 48.

A good hotel not far from the Collection Guggenheim, in one of the quietest parts of Venice. Some of the rooms overlook a charming *rio*, but the decor is unexceptional.

### Pausania★★★

Fondamenta Gherardini, 2824 (*vaporetto* 1, Ca' Rezzonico)
☎ 041 522 20 83
🖷 041 522 29 89.

A 14th-century palace beside a *fondamenta* where market-garden boats are moored. The outside staircase resembles that of Goldoni's house. Very quiet.

### Agli Alboretti★★

(see p. 49).

### Seguso★★

Zattere, 779 (*vaporetti* 52 and 82, Zattere)
☎ 041 528 68 58
🖷 041 522 23 40.

A small guesthouse with a view of the Rio S. Vio and Canale della Giudecca, plus fine furniture, embroidered tablecloths, stucco ceilings, Venetian chandeliers, and a garden.

### Locanda Ca' Foscari★

Calle della Frescada, 3887/B (*vaporetti* 1 and 82, S. Tomà)
☎ 041 71 04 01
🖷 041 71 08 17
Closed Dec. and Jan.

A pleasant and inexpensive guesthouse in the S. M. Gloriosa dei Frari district. The vast, light-filled rooms overlooking a courtyard or garden are always well-kept but few have en-suite bathrooms.

## Sestieri of Santa Croce and San Polo

### Marconi★★★

Fondamenta del Vin, 729 S. Polo (*vaporetto* 1, S. Silvestro)
☎ 041 522 20 68
🖷 041 522 87 00.

A splendid residence with rooms overlooking the Grand Canal. If you like wood panelling and Rococo decoration, then this congenial hotel is for you.

### San Cassiano★★★

Calle della Rosa, 2232 S. Croce (*vaporetto* 1, S. Stae)
☎ 041 524 17 68
🖷 041 72 10 33.

A 14th-century palace in a district rich in authentic restaurants. Its Oriental carpets, coffered ceilings and lounges with a view of the Ca' d'Oro make it the finest Venetian palace.

### Doni★

Calle del Vin, 4656 (*vaporetti* 1, 14, 52 and 82, S. Zaccaria)
☎ 041 522 42 67.

You'll get a smiling welcome at this 16th-century house behind Piazza S. Marco, in the peace and quiet of the Rio del Vin. The rooms with arched windows overlook a garden or a small *rio*. Only two of them have en-suite bathrooms though.

## Sestiere of Cannaregio

### Eden★★★
**Rio terrà della Maddalena, 2357 (*vaporetti* 1 and 82, S. Marcuola)
☎ 041 524 40 03
🖷 041 72 02 28.**

A small, authentic Venetian hotel overlooking a courtyard with an old well. On top of this, it's reasonably priced and in a district full of *osterie* (inns). What more could you ask for?

### Malibran★★★
**Salizzada S. Giovanni Crisostomo, 5864 (*vaporetti* 1 and 82, Cannaregio)
☎ 041 522 80 28
🖷 041 523 92 43.**

An old house near the Ponte di Rialto, in the quiet square that's home to the Malibran theatre. Cosy rooms with 18th-century furniture and pink damask walls.

## The Giudecca

### Cipriani★★★★
**Zitelle, 10 (*vaporetti* 52 and 82, Guidecca)
☎ 041 520 77 44
🖷 041 520 77 45.**

One of Venice's largest hotels (and also the most expensive), with luxurious rooms, a sea water swimming pool to cool off in and a high-class restaurant. A must (if you can afford it!).

HOTEL RISTORANTE
## MALIBRAN
★ ★ ★

# RESTAURANTS

## Sestiere of San Marco

### Antico Martini★★★★

**Campo S. Fantin, 1983**
(**vaporetto 1,**
**S. Maria del Giglio)**
☎ **041 522 41 21.**

Ultra-sophisticated cuisine to savour by candlelight on a terrace at the foot of La Fenice. Try the sole Martini or the fillet of duck breast with truffles and enjoy one of the 300 wines from the cellar.

### Harry's Bar★★★★

**Calle Vallaresso, 1323**
(**vaporetti 1 and 82,**
**S. Marco)**
☎ **041 528 57 77**
**Open every day.**

Possibly the best restaurant in Venice (and the most expensive), but somewhere you should try to visit at least once in your life. Everything is excellent here, but if you're spoilt for choice, try the *carpaccio* – it's exquisite.

### La Caravella★★★★

**Via XXII Marzo, 2399**
(**vaporetti 1 and 82,**
**S. Marco)**
☎ **041 520 89 01**
**Open every day.**

High-class cuisine in a tasteful and distinguished setting. La Caravella has reinvented the art of preparing fish; make sure you try the lobster soup which is quite delicious.

### Alla Colomba★★

**Piscina di Frezzeria, 1665**
(**vaporetti 1 and 82,**
**S. Marco)**
☎ **041 522 11 75**
**Closed Wed. lunchtime.**

Another unusual place, which resembles a museum (Chagall, De Chirico, Carrà and Poliakoff all paid for their meals with paintings). Try the pasta and white bean soup (*pasta con fagioli*).

### Al Graspo de Ua★★★

**Calle dei Bombasseri, 5094**
(**vaporetti 1 and 82,**
**Rialto)**
☎ **041 520 01 50 or**
**041 522 36 47**
**closed Mon.**

One of the best fish restaurants in the lagoon has opened in this former sacristy. The owner goes shopping every morning and has the reputation of being very fussy about freshness. The soup is excellent.

### Trattoria do Forni★★★

**Calle Specchieri, 457-468**
(**vaporetti 1 and 82,**
**S. Marco and Rialto)**
☎ **041 523 21 48**
**Open every day.**

A tourist restaurant but excellent nonetheless. In summer you can savour the house speciality of *rombo* (turbot) with olives, outside in the cool of the evening.

### Al Bacaretto★★

**Salizzada S. Samuele and**
**Calle Crosera, 3447**
(**vaporetto 82, S. Marco)**
☎ **041 528 93 36**
**Closed Sun. and Mon. even.**

A typical trattoria that's always full to bursting and only a stone's throw from Palazzo Grassi. Simple traditional dishes.

### Al Teatro★★

(see p. 41).

### Antica Carbonera★★

(see p. 47).

### Alle Colonette★

**Rio terrà delle Colonette,**
**987** (**vaporetti 1 and 82,**
**S. Marco)**
**Open every day exc. Wed. in**
**winter, noon-3pm, 7-10pm**
☎ **041 523 70 82.**

Another inexpensive restaurant in the most touristy part of the district. Sample the tasty Venetian specialities while sitting at the bar.

## Fiore★★

**Calle delle Botteghe, 3461**
**(*vaporetto* 1, S. Angelo)**
**☎ 041 523 53 10**
**Closed Tue.**

There are always lots of people and a lively atmosphere in this pleasant *osteria* near Campo S. Stefano. Sip an *ombra* (small glass of wine) at the bar while you wait for a table.

## Haig's Grill★★

**S. M. del Giglio, 2477**
**S. Marco (*vaporetto* 1,**
**S. M. del Giglio)**
**☎ 041 528 94 56.**

It's not the cuisine that's unusual about this place, (it's an American restaurant), but

the fact you can eat here from 10 pm until 5 in the morning).

## Vini da Arturo★★

(see p. 45).

## A la Campana★

**Calle dei Fabbri, 4720**
**(*vaporetti* 1 and 82,**
**S. Marco or Rialto)**
**☎ 041 528 51 70**
**Closed Sun. in winter.**

An authentic and inexpensive little *osteria* where you can sample real Venetian dishes with the locals. You'll get a very warm welcome.

## Da Ivo★★

**Ramo dei Fuseri, 1809**
**(*vaporetti* 1 and 82,**
**S. Marco)**
**☎ 041 528 50 04**
**Closed Sun.**

This romantic little restaurant beside a *rio* specialises in grilled meat and fish (cooked over olive wood charcoal, no less). Authentic Venetian atmosphere and friendly service.

## Al Profeta★★

**Calle Lunga S. Barnaba, 2671 Dorsoduro (*vaporetto* 1, Ca' Rezzonico)**
☎ 041 523 74 66
**closed Sun.**

A pleasant and very charming little trattoria. The new management has opted for 'seasonal' cuisine that allows you to savour the freshest and finest produce of the region.

## Alla Riveta

**Ponte S. Provolo 4625 (*vaporetti* 1, 52 and 82, S. Zaccaria)**
☎ 041 528 73 02
**Closed Mon.**

This typical little restaurant is a good place to get an idea of the variety of Venetian food, especially the fish-based dishes. *Polpette* (meatballs), *folpetti* (which horrifyingly enough are dormice) are all on offer at the bar. The place is frequented by gondoliers.

### Sestiere of Dorsoduro

## Agli Alboretti★★★

(see p. 49).

## Linea d'Ombra★★★

(see p. 51).

## Antica Locanda Montin★★

**Fondamenta delle Eremite, 1147 (*vaporetti* 1 and 82, Accademia; 52 and 82, Zattere)**
☎ 041 522 33 07
**Closed Tue. even. and Wed.**

This good trattoria decorated with modern paintings was once the haunt of students and intellectuals, but they've now made way for tour groups. The service isn't always up to scratch but the garden is very pleasant in summer.

## Ai Cugnai★

**Calle Nuova Sant'Agnese, 857 (*vaporetti* 1 and 82, San Vio. Dorsoduro)**
☎ 041 528 92 38
**Closed Mon.**

Since it was praised in the columns of a French magazine (the article is naturally displayed on the door), this nicely decorated restaurant run by three sisters has been much frequented by visitors from France. It's a good place to have lunch after visiting the Museo dell'Accademia.

## San Basilio★

(see p. 53).

NOI CONSIGLIA

SCAMPI con FAGIOLI e RUCOLA   24000
POLIPETTI AL POMODORO   20000
INSALATA D. PESCE   24000
INSALATA DI FUNGHI   22000
GAMBERETTI ALLO LIMONE   28000
FUNGHI AI FERRI
TAGLIOLINI CON TARTUFO   29000
    BIANCO D'ALBA
SPAGHETTI CON GAMBERONI   24000
    POMODORO E BASILICO
FEGATO DI VITELLO   28000
    ALLA VENEZIANA
BRANZINO AL CARBONE   33000
MOLECCHE FRITTE   32000

tempting array that you can then eat amid the wine bottles, or else opt for a simple, well-prepared meal in the restaurant.

## Da Ignazio ★

**Calle Saoneri, 2749 S. Polo (*vaporetti* 1 and 82, S. Tomà)**
**☎ 041 523 48 52**
**closed Sat. and late July.**

A trattoria where you can have a leisurely dinner under a vine. The cuisine is good and the tiramisù melts in your mouth.

## Do Mori ★

**(see p. 55).**

## Vivaldi ★

**Calle della Madonnetta, 1457 S. Polo (*vaporetto* 1, S. Silvestro)**
**☎ 041 523 81 85**
**closed Sun. in summer.**

You'll find good Venetian wines, skilfully cooked Venetian specialities and excellent fish dishes in this *osteria* dedicated to the 'red priest'. Moderate prices in a select setting.

## Sestiere of San Polo

## Antiche Carampane ★★★

**Rio terrà de la Carampane, 1911 (*vaporetto* 1, S. Silvestro)**
**☎ 041 524 01 65**
**closed Sun., Mon. and Aug.**

This charming fish restaurant is elegant and refined and the cuisine is simply delicious. You could try prawns accompanied by a smooth polenta, followed by sea bass cooked in parcels and a bottle of the house white wine. Enjoy your meal!

## Poste Vecie ★★★

**(see p. 55).**

## Alla Patatina ★

**(see p. 57).**

## Osteria Antico Dolo ★

**San Polo 778 (*vaporetto* 1, S. Silvestro)**
**☎ 041 522 65 46**
**Closed Sun.**

You can sample typical Venetian cuisine here composed entirely of fresh fish. It's the ideal place for a light meal. There's a good choice of local wines and you can expect a very friendly welcome.

## Do Spade ★

**Calle do Spade, 860 S. Polo (*vaporetti* 1 and 82, Rialto)**
**☎ 041 521 05 74**
**closed Sun., Thu. even. and out of season.**

Another *osteria* that's retained its charm despite the proximity of the tourist-ridden Ponte di Rialto. You can have either choose a sandwich from a

## Sestiere of Santa Croce

## Nono Risorto ★★

**Sottoportego della Signora Bettina, 2338 (*vaporetti* 1 and 82, Rialto)**
**☎ 041 524 11 69**
**closed Wed. and Jan.**

Always packed, this restaurant is particularly pleasant in summer, when you can dine under a wisteria beside the *rio*. The pizzas are said to be the best in Venice. Don't miss the *speck-zucca* (raw ham with pumpkin) in season. The service tends to vary according to the owner's mood.

## Alla Zucca ★

**Ponte del Megio, 1762 (*vaporetto* 1, S. Stae)**
**☎ 041 524 15 70**
**Closed Sun.**

A delightful little restaurant that serves tasty pasta and vegetarian dishes. There's a terrace that's ideal in the summer, where you can have lunch or dinner under a parasol, far from the noise of the city.

## Al Ponte★

**Ponte del Megio, 1666**
**(*vaporetto* 1, S. Stae)**
**☎ 041 71 97 77**
**Closed Sun. (exc. festivals)**
**and Aug.**

This unpretentious trattoria in a district little frequented by tourists is an excellent place to eat fried fish. Don't miss the cabbage soup (*castradina*) during the Festa della Salute.

### Sestiere of Castello

## Corte Sconta★★★

**Calle del Pestrin, 3886**
**(*vaporetto* 1, Arsenale)**
**☎ 041 522 70 24**
**Closed Sun.-Mon., late Jul.-**
**early Aug. and Jan.**

A chic, trendy trattoria off the beaten tourist track (near the Arsenal tratorria). Gleaming wooden furniture, a magnificent copper bar and, above all, excellent fish dishes, although big eaters may find the portions a little meagre. In fine weather the tables are set up in the courtyard.

## Al Mascaron★★

**Calle Lunga S. M. Formosa,**
**5225 (*vaporetti* 1, 14, 52**
**and 82, S. Zaccaria)**
**☎ 041 522 59 95**
**closed Sun.**

An authentic Venetian trattoria decorated with enormous wine flasks next to the church of S. M. Formosa. *Pasta e fagioli* (pasta with white beans) and absolutely delicious grilled fish.

## Da Aciugheta★

(see p. 59).

### Sestiere of Cannaregio

## Ca' d'Oro★★

**Ramo Ca' d'Oro, 3912**
**(*vaporetto* 1, Ca d'Oro)**
**☎ 041 528 53 24**
**Closed Thu., Sun. lunch and**
**Aug.**

'Alla Vedova' (The Widow's Place), as the Venetians call it, is a lively trattoria that never empties. In an original 19th-century setting, you can sample *bacalà* that's among the best in Venice.

## Ai Promessi Sposi★

**Calle dell'Oca, 4367**
**(*vaporetto* 1, Ca' d'Oro)**
**☎ 041 522 86 09**
**Closed Wed.**

This irresistible trattoria, tucked away in a tiny alleyway, still hasn't been discovered by tourists. Come here to sample all sorts of delicious dishes (such as clams and fish pie) or simply to have a bite at the bar.

## All'Antica Adelaide★

**Calle Priuli, 3728**
**(*vaporetto* 1, Ca' d'Oro)**
**☎ 041 520 34 51**
**closed Mon.**

Tina Dainese welcomes you with a smile to her typically Venetian trattoria, only a stone's throw from Strada Nova. In an easy-going and fun student atmosphere, you can try spaghetti with clams and veal's liver cooked the Venetian way, all washed down with a jug of white wine.

## Antiche Cantine Ardenghi★

(see p. 61).

*The Hotel Cipriani on the Giudecca*

A fish restaurant in a medieval palace next to the church of S. Pietro. Many tourists come here in season, but it offers good value for money.

## Barada★

(see p. 63).

## Bentigodi★

Calle Sele, 1418-1424
(*vaporetti* 1 and 82, S. Marcuola)
☎ 041 71 62 69
closed Sun.

Good home cooking is served at this charming little trattoria. Order pea soup and delicious *gnocchi* at the bar, and wash it all down with the usual jug of Italian white wine.

## The Giudecca

## Harry's Dolci★★★

(see pp. 65, 122).

## Cipriani★★★★

Zitelle, 10 (*vaporetti* 52 and 82, Zitelle)
☎ 041 520 77 44
closed in winter.

A high-class restaurant for the residents of the hotel Cipriani (see p. 75), but also for food-lovers who flock to the Giudecca to sample inventive, superbly presented cuisine. There's a marvellous view from the restaurant as well.

## Iguana★★

(see p. 65).

## Murano

## Trattoria Valmarena★★★

Fondamenta Navagero, 31
(*vaporetti* 12, 13, 14 and 52, Museo-Murano)
☎ 041 73 93 13
Closed Wed., even. out of season and Jan.

The best restaurant on Murano has a pleasant garden in summer in which to sample *rombo* (turbot), the house speciality.

## Ai Frati★★

(see p. 67).

## Busa alla Tore★★

Campo S. Stefano, 3
(*vaporetti* 12, 13, 14 and 52, Museo-Murano)
☎ 041 73 96 62
Closed in the evening.

## Burano and Torcello

## Locanda Cipriani★★★

(Torcello; see p. 69).

## Da Romano★★★

(Burano; see p. 69).

## Al Gatto Nero★★

Fondamenta Giudecca, 88
Burano (*vaporetti* 12 and 14, Burano)
☎ 041 73 01 20
Closed Mon. and late Oct.-early Nov.

Less busy than the previous restaurant and, above all, less expensive. The setting is pleasant (the restaurant is decorated with paintings), the service is good, if a little distant, and the fish dishes are all excellent.

# CAFÉS AND ICE-CREAM PARLOURS

*pierini* – tiny moreish toasted cheese and ham sandwiches.

## Florian
(see p. 39).

## Lavena
**Piazza S. Marco, 133
(*vaporetti* 1 and 82, S. Marco)
☎ 041 522 40 70
closed Tue. in winter.**

A plush tea-room founded in 1750 to rival its neighbours, the Florian and the Quadri. With its mirrors, 18th-century atmosphere and memories of Richard Wagner, who was a frequent visitor, the Lavena is one of the great cafés of the square.

## CAFÉS

### Sestiere of San Marco

### Alle Botteghe
**Calle delle Botteghe, 3454
(*vaporetto* 1, S. Angelo)
☎ 041 522 81 81
Closed Sat. afternoon and Sun.**

A real Venetian bar that's a pleasant place to have a beer or some kind of spritz (Venetian aperitif) accompanied by a variety of sandwiches.

### Dal Col
**Calle dei Fabbri, 1035
(*vaporetti* 1 and 82, Rialto)
☎ 041 520 55 29
Closed Sun.**

A café-pâtisserie where you can take a break from shopping and enjoy a slice of apple tart or a croissant with a creamy cappuccino.

### Harry's Bar
**Calle Vallaresso, 1323
(*vaporetti* 1 and 82, S. Marco)
☎ 041 523 57 77
Open every day.**

If you were alarmed by the restaurant prices, you can console yourself with a cocktail at Harry's Bar. There are two absolute musts – the Rossini (strawberry juice and champagne, only in season) and the Bellini (peach juice and champagne). Drink them with

## Quadri (see p. 39).

## Rosa Salva
(see p. 98).

### Sestiere of Dorsoduro

### Da Gino
**Piscina Forner, 855/A
(*vaporetti* 1 and 82, Accademia)
Closed Sun.**

This is very much a locals' bar. Along with the television and

grappa, there are a few seats, which is pretty rare in Venice!

## Il Caffè

Campo S. Margherita, 2963
(*vaporetto* 1, Ca' Rezzonico)
☎ 041 528 79 98
closed Sun.

A delightful little café with a 1900s decor. The antique coffee percolator inside still works.

### Sestiere of Castello

## Birreria Forst

Calle delle Rasse, 4540
(*vaporetti* 1, 12, 13, 14, 52
and 82, S. Zaccaria)
☎ 041 523 05 57
Closed Sat.

A small café in the pleasant Castello district where you can stop for a bite to eat between museum visits. There's a choice of *tramezzini piccanti* (triangular spicy sandwiches on wholemeal bread), a plate of *porchetta* (roasted suckling pig) and lots more besides.

### Sestiere of Cannaregio

## Al Giubagiò

Fondamente Nuove, 5039
(*vaporetti* 12, 13 and 52,
Fondamente Nuove)
☎ 041 523 60 84.

If you're waiting for a *vaporetto* to take you to the islands (Murano, Burano and Torcello), here's a place well off the beaten tourist track where you can have a drink in an atmosphere that's entirely Venetian.

### Giudecca

## Harry's Dolci

(see p. 65).

# ICE-CREAM PARLOURS

## Causin Renato

Campo S. Margherita,
2996 Dorsoduro
(*vaporetto* 1, Ca' Rezzonico)
☎ 041 523 60 91
closed Sat. and Aug.

An old-fashioned shop that's home to one of the best traditional ice-cream makers in Venice. The house speciality is the aptly-named 'sublime ice cream'. In summer, the tables are set out in Campo S. Margherita.

## Gelateria Nico

(see p. 49).

## Il Doge

Campo S. Margherita,
3058/A Dorsoduro
(*vaporetto* 1, Ca' Rezzonico)
☎ 041 523 46 07.

An interesting choice of over forty flavours and reasonable prices too, in one of the most delightful *campi* in Venice.

## Il Gelatone

Viale Santa Maria
Elisabetta,

63/A Lido (*vaporetti* 1, 6,
14, 52 and 82, Lido)
☎ 041 526 56 46
Closed Mon.

The best ice-cream parlour on the Lido. The *mangia e bevi* (eat and drink) ice cream with fruit and cream is quite delicious after a swim in summer or between films at the Mostra.

## Rosa Salva

(see p. 98).

## San Stefano

(see p. 43).

A    B

**1**

S. ALVISE

MADONNA DELL'ORTO

*Rio di S. Alvise*

*Rio di San Girolamo*

**Chiesa della
Madonna dell'Orto**

*Canale di Cannaregio*

*Rio della Misericordia*

*Sacca
della
Misericordia*

**S. Giobbe**

*Rio Terrà
S. Leonardo*

*Canale della
Misericordia*

*Str. di Noale*

**Chiesa
dei Gesuiti**

FOND.
NUOVE

S. MARCUOLA

*Canal*

*Grande*

**Palazzo
Pesaro**

**Ca' d'Oro**

*Nuova*

**SS. Apostoli**

MESTRE

**Stazione
Santa Lucia**

*Rio Marin*

**S. Giacomo
dell'Orio**

CA' D'ORO

FERROVIA

**Ch. di Maria
dei Miracoli**

*Rio*

**Autorimessa**

P

**PIAZZALE
ROMA**

P

P

**Chiesa
dei Frari**

CAMPO DI
SAN POLO

*Grande*

PONTE
DI RIALTO

RIALTO

*Calle dei Fabbri*

**2**

*Nuovo*

*Canal*

*Rio di S. Margherita*

*Rio Ca' Foscari*

CAMPO
SANTA
MARGHERITA

**Ca'
Rezzonico**

S. TOMÀ

*Grande*

CAMPO
SAN
ANGELO

CAMPO
MANIN

**S. Marc**

**Palazzo
Ducale**

PIAZZA
S. MARCO

*Rio di S. Barnaba*

CA' REZZONICO

**S. Stefano**

PIAZZETTA

**S. Sebastiano**

ACCADEMIA

**S. Trovaso**

**Galleria
dell'Accademia**

*Canal*

S. MARIA
DEL GIGLIO

*Grande*

S. MARCO
VALLARESSA

S. MARCO
GIARDINETT

S. BASILIO

*Canale*

**Gesuati**

ZATTERE

ZATTERE-
TRAGHETTO

**Pal. Venier
dei Leoni**

**S. Maria
della Salute**

*Punta
della Dogana*

Fusina

*Can. dei Lavraneri*

**Spirito
Santo**

**3**

*della*

*Giudecca*

S. EUFEMIA

GIUDECCA-
TRAGHETTO

ZITELLE

**Chiesa
delle
Zitelle**

**S. Eufemia**

REDENTORE

CAMPO
DI MARTE

**S. Cosmo**

*R. d. Ponte Longo*

**Chiesa del
Redentore**

*GIUDECCA*

A    B

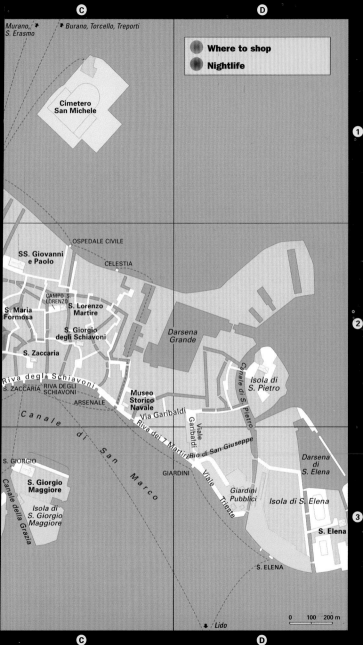

# Shopping Practicalities

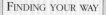

**T**utto è possibile a Venezia – everything's possible in Venice – as everyone in the shops will be quick to tell you. You can buy a piece of lacquered furniture, order a personalised Carnival mask or a copy of your favourite painting by Canaletto, fall for a Murano glass chandelier and have it shipped home, or whatever else takes your fancy – business sense comes naturally in a city that built its wealth on trade.

## FINDING YOUR WAY

**N**ext to each address in the Shopping and Nightlife sections we have given its location on the map of Venice on pp. 84-85.

## OPENING TIMES – A VENETIAN MYSTERY

As a rule, the shops in Venice open every day except Sunday (and sometimes Monday morning) from 9/9.30am to 1pm and from 3/3.30pm to 7 or even 8pm. But these times are only intended as a rough guide – this is Italy and opening times vary according to the season, the kind of shop and even the mood of the shopkeeper (especially in the case of craftsmen, who may leave a sign saying *chiuso* when they feel like getting some fresh air). Over the Christmas period, at Carnival time and in summer, the mask and Murano glass shops, and tourist shops in general, open on Sundays and don't always close for the sacrosanct midday break any more.

In other words, if you really want to buy something in a particular shop, the best thing to do is to telephone in advance and enquire about opening times (those shown in the following pages can vary). Another possibility is to come on Saturday, when shopping is in full swing, between 4 and 8pm.

## ANNUAL CLOSING

This usually takes place in August but can also occur in January, shortly before the Carnival.

## A SUGGESTED ROUTE

From Piazza San Marco, make your way through

the Mercerie to the Rialto, then take the 82 *vaporetto* to S. Samuele. Once you get there, make your way to Campo S. Stefano, then go back to where you started via Campo S. M. del Giglio and Calle Larga XXII Marzo, the home of luxury shopping.

## CREDIT CARDS, TRAVELLER'S CHEQUES AND EUROCHEQUES

Thanks to tourism, payment by credit card (VISA, MASTERCARD, AMERICAN EXPRESS and DINER'S) is widespread in Venice. Most smart shops also take Eurocheques and traveller's cheques, though here, as elsewhere, the rate of exchange is unfavourable.

Because of this, it's a good idea to change your traveller's cheques at a bank before you set off for the shops (or take traveller's cheques in lire). But the simplest thing to do is to pay by card.

## SALES

These take place in January and July, from the second week in the month onwards, as laid down by Italian law. Look out for the signs saying *sconti* or *saldi*.

## PRICES

Bear in mind that Venice is the most expensive city in Italy. However, no-one will try to pull the wool over your eyes and prices are displayed everywhere, except where it would be considered bad taste (in luxury jewellers', for example). Bargaining isn't a possibility, except at the Campo S. Maurizio antique market (see p. 43).

## ORDERS AND BULKY OBJECTS

If you've set your heart on Venetian velvet curtains, a made-to-measure Fortuny fabric dress, 12 bottles of *Prosecco*, a Murano glass chandelier or a varnished wooden speedboat and can afford it, nothing could be simpler. The Venetian shopkeepers will see to everything – they'll arrange despatch and take care of any insurance formalities. To give an idea of price, it costs around L50,000 to ship home an average-sized Murano glass vase and takes about a fortnight, while a chandelier costs twice as much and takes one to two months.

The following is a reliable transport company:

**Sattis** :
Zattere, 1493 Dorsoduro
☎ 041 520 49 77.

## CUSTOMS

For citizens of the European Union, there are no customs formalities to complete. You simply have to produce an invoice showing that duty was paid on the goods in Italy. As a rule, you need the authorisation of the Belli Arti, the Italian equivalent of the National Heritage, to export objects over fifty years old and you may be asked to show the permit and invoice when you go through customs.

Beware of buying the fake goods (luggage, perfume, etc.) that you're offered in the evening. Besides being poor imitations, they may land you with a hefty fine.

## OPEN ON SUNDAY

If you want to go shopping on Sunday, try exploring the San Marco district. The clothes, jewellery, glass and souvenir shops of every kind open virtually all year round.

# FROM *LEGATORIA* TO *LEGATORIA*

## FROM PEN TO PAPER

If you want to take home a typically Venetian souvenir that's both chic and inexpensive, stationery is ideal. Just step inside one of the many tiny *legatorie*, of the Serenissima and you'll find stationery of every kind – and can also watch real craftsmen at work, perhaps recalling childhood memories of the smell of paper and ink.

### SESTIERE OF SAN MARCO

#### Gonzalez

Calle della Fenice, 1854
(*vaporetto* 1,
S. M. del Giglio-B2)
☎ 041 528 55 63
Ev. day exc. Sun.
10am-7.30pm.

A friendly craftsman who sells all kinds of stationery, from traditional writing paper to imitation panther- and zebra-skin diaries and note-books for around L30,000. The shop window alone is worth seeing.

#### Paolo Olbi

Calle Mandola, 3653
(*vaporetto* 1, S. Angelo-B2)
☎ 041 528 50 25
Ev. day exc. Sun. and Mon.
morn. 10am-12.30pm,
3.30-7.30pm.

A *legatoria* where you'll find pencils, leather-bound diaries, photograph albums and sketchpads covered in marbled paper. You can also have a stamp made with the design of your choice for a very reasonable price.

#### Il Papiro

Calle del Piovan, 2764
(*vaporetto* 1,
S. M. del Giglio-B2)
☎ 041 522 30 55
Ev. day 10am-7.30pm.

Diaries and other notebooks covered in marbled paper, as well as more original stationery for young and old alike, all at affordable prices, including pens, seals, coloured pencils and very attractive greetings cards.

#### Legatoria Piazzesi

S. M. del Giglio, 2511/C

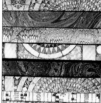

(*vaporetto* 1,
S. M. del Giglio-B2)
☎ 041 522 12 02
Ev. day exc. Sun.
10am-1pm, 4-7pm.

Make a visit to the oldest *legatoria* in Venice a matter of priority, even

though the prices are high. It's a marvellous shop with an endless variety of original binding paper and expensive but gorgeous boxes covered in marbled paper, as well as

snakes and ladders sets, playing cards, tarot cards and papier mâché Commedia dell'Arte figurines.

## Alberto Valese

**Campiello S. Stefano, 3471 (*vaporetto* 1, S. Angelo; *vaporetto* 82, S. Samuele-B2)**
☎ 041 520 09 21
Ev. day exc. Sun.
10am-7pm in season.

Along with the Legatoria Piazzesi, this is the other great marbled paper specialist you really mustn't miss. Alberto Valese reproduces his original patterns on a multitude of objects, including notebooks, boxes and small papier mâché drawers, as well as silk and crêpe de Chine scarves. You may see one of his workers

making floral prints (*Ebrû* in Turkish) using special techniques in the back room.

## SESTIERE OF SAN POLO

### Luna Edizioni d'Arte

**Campo S. Cassiano, 1856 (*vaporetto* 1, S. Stae-B2)**
☎ 041 524 40 22
Ev. day 10.30am-7.30pm.

A shop like a doll's house, where you can buy all kinds of notebooks at all kinds of prices. You can also order personalised labels for your home-made wines.

### Legatoria Polliero

**Campo dei Frari, 2995 (A/B2 *vaporetti* 1 and 82, S. Tomà)**
☎ 041 528 51 30
Ev. day exc. Sun.
10.30am-1pm, 3.30-7.30pm.

This tiny *legatoria* in the shadow of the gigantic church of the Frari has marvellous marbled-paper objects, from small pocket diaries to large desk diaries. You may be able to have your favourite small book bound for around L80,000 and you can even have it sent home.

### Roba di Katia

**Ruga Vecchia, 788 (*vaporetti* 1 and 82, Rialto-B2)**
☎ 041 523 19 49

**Every day exc. Sun.**
**10am-1pm, 3-7.30pm.**

You're sure to fall for Roba di Katia's very inexpensive notebooks or for the tiny mini-diaries costing a very reasonable L10,000.

# AROUND THE FABRIC SHOPS

## VELVETS, SILKS AND FORTUNY FABRICS

The fabric shops of Venice are the true guardians of Italian style. It's their silks, velvets and damasks that Venetian aristocrats buy when they want to change the hangings in their drawing rooms. It's to them that the Italian state turns to when it decides to restore the inside of a palace. However, you'll need to have fairly deep pockets if you want to feature alongside the illustrious names in their order books.

### SESTIERE OF SAN MARCO

#### Mario Bevilacqua

Fondamenta Canonica, 337/B (*vaporetti* 1 and 52, S. Zaccaria-C2)
☎ 041 528 75 81
Every day 9.30am-7.30pm.

Don't miss this shop – it's a work of art in itself. You'll be able to realise all your decorative dreams here, as long as you're prepared to splash out – a metre/yard of fabric costs hundreds of thousands of lire. If you're looking for a marginally cheaper gift, you might consider the little fabric purses (L200,000).

#### Gaggio

Campo S. Stefano, 3451 (*vaporetto* 1, S. Samuele-B2)
☎ 041 522 85 74
Every day exc. Sun. 9.30am-1pm, 3.30-7.30pm.

A well-known shop that specialises in silk and printed velvet inspired by Art Deco drawings and Fortuny designs (see p. 16). You'll also find accessories for around L300,000 here.

#### Lorenzo Rubelli

Campo S. Gallo, 1089 (*vaporetto* 1, S. Marco-B2)
☎ 041 523 61 10
Every day exc. Sat. and Sun. 8.30am-12.30pm, 3.30-7.30pm.

This shop is an institution that produces tiny amounts of sumptuous hand-woven damask and velvet. Its extraordinary hand-stamped

velvet is used to decorate Venetian palaces. The head office of this illustrious house is Palazzo Corner Spinelli (S. Angelo, 3877 ☎ 041 521 64 11).

## Trois

**Campo S. Maurizio, 2660 (*vaporetto* 1, S. M. del Giglio-B2) ☎ 041 522 29 05 Every day exc. Sun. and Mon. morn. 10am-1pm, 4-7.30pm.**

The only place in Venice where you can buy the famous Fortuny fabrics. But at L330,000 a metre/yard, you risk ruin if you want to turn your home into a Venetian palace.

## Venetia Studium

**Via XXII Marzo 2425 (workshop) or Mercerie 723 (*vaporetti* 1, 52 and 82, S. Zaccaria, or 1 and 82, Rialto-B2) and S. Marco 2403 (*vaporetto* 1, S. M. del Giglio-B2) (shops) ☎ 041 522 92 81 ☎ 041 522 73 53 Every day 9.30am-8pm, Sun. 10.30am-7.30pm.**

More Fortuny-inspired silk and velvet. The price of the scarves, which are absolutely gorgeous, starts at L300,000 and goes sky-high. The Fortuny lamps are fantastic and there are pretty purses for L200,000. You can visit the workshops if you like.

## SESTIERE OF SAN POLO

### Color Casa
**Campo S. Polo, 1989–1990**

> ### QUICK GUIDE TO VENETIAN FABRICS
>
> **Brocade, damask and taffeta**
> ■ Brocade: embossed silk fabric, often containing a large amount of gold and silver thread.
> ■ Damask: silk fabric with the same pattern appearing on the right side (in satin on a taffeta background) and the wrong side (in taffeta on a satin background).
> ■ Taffeta: silk with a plain weave.
>
> **Artificial and natural silk**
> When it comes in contact with fire, natural silk burns slowly without flames. Artificial silk flares up and is quickly consumed by fire.
>
> **Care of velvet**
> Velvet loses its sheen with wear. You can restore its suppleness by wetting it on the wrong side and holding it over a hot iron (being careful not to let them touch), then leaving it to dry in the air.

**(*vaporetto* 1, S. Silvestro-B2) ☎ 041 523 60 71 Every day exc. Sun. (Aug.-Nov.) 9am-1pm, 3-7pm.**

Very chic fabric to make scarves, throws and bedspreads. The scarves and shawls on display in the window are gorgeous but expensive (around L300,000). The assistants are friendly and very helpful.

### Valeria Bellinaso
**Campo S. Aponal 1226 (*vaporetto* 1, S. Silvestro-B2) ☎ 041 522 33 51 Every day exc. Sun. in winter 10am-1.30pm, 3.30-7.30pm.**

In Valeria's shop, you can get lost among all the silk and velvet in the form of stoles, hats, scarves, sunshades and shoes. The designs, which are all original, are made exclusively for the shop by craftsmen. You'll be surprised by the interesting and unusual combinations of colours.

### Pasinetti
**Campiello Ca' Bernardo, 1321 (*vaporetto* 1, S. Silvestro-B2) ☎ 041 522 32 65 ☎ 041 522 88 21 Every day exc. Sat. and Sun. 9am-noon, 3-6pm.**

The illustrious house of Pasinetti, which is housed in the Palazzo Bernardi, sells fabrics of breathtaking beauty.

# CARNIVAL TIME

## CARNIVAL MASKS AND COSTUMES

There seem to be hundreds of Carnival shops in Venice, perhaps almost too many. In an effort to mark themselves out from peddlers of mass-produced masks, the best Venetian craftsmen show great ingenuity, constantly racking their brains to invent new masks – after all, there's nothing worse than turning up in the same disguise as the next person!

### SESTIERE OF DORSODURO

**Mondonovo Maschere**

Di Lovato Guerrino
Dorsoduro, 3063 (*vaporetto* 1, Ca'Rezzonico-B2)
☎ 041 52 87 344
☎ 041 52 12 633
Every day exc. Sun. 10am-7pm.

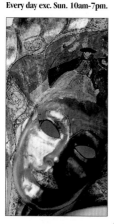

This is where the artists of the Commedia dell'Arte theatre come to order their masks. The shop and workshop near Campo S. Margherita is worth more than a quick visit. You'll find more than 300 masks here, at a wide range of prices and to suit all tastes.

### SESTIERE OF CASTELLO

**La Bottega d'Arte-Il Cignoca**

Calle limeto la Sacrestia, 4361 (*vaporetti* 1, 52 and 82, S. Zaccaria-C2)
☎ 041 45 33 63
Every day 10.30am-7.30pm.

You'll find masks at very good prices in this shop near Piazza San Marco, especially gilded masks for under L50,000. There's plenty of choice of both papier mâché and leather masks too. It you are interested, the craftsman will explain the various steps involved in making the masks.

**Renzo Marega**

Fondamenta dell'Osmarin, 4968 (*vaporetti* 1, 52 and 82, S. Zaccaria-C2)
☎ 041 522 30 36
Every day 10.30am-7.30pm.

Surprisingly low prices and a warm welcome make this one of the best places in the centre of Venice to buy a mask made in the traditional way (from under L40,000 for a papier mâché mask to over L100,000 for a leather one). You'll also find inexpensive necklaces and reproductions of Commedia dell'Arte characters in this colourful little shop lined with pretty bottles.

**Papier mâohó**

Calle Lunga S. M. Formosa, Castello 5175 (*vaporetti* 1 and 82, Rialto-C2)
☎ 041 522 99 95
Every day exc. Mon. 9am-7.30pm.

This elegant shop, resembling an art gallery, sells not only very ornate masks but also beautiful hand-painted ceramics.

Everything is attractively priced and the assistants will offer you good advice.

## La Venexiana Atelier

**Ponte Canonica, 4322**
(*vaporetti* 1, 52 and 82,
S. Zaccaria-C2)
☎ and ❻ 041 523 35 58
**Every day 9.30am-7pm**
(11pm in summer).

A very nice shop that's worth a look in itself, with an excellent craftsman specialising in traditional hand-painted papier mâché masks. La Venexiana Atelier also has Carnival clothes and pretty, old-fashioned dolls.

### *SESTIERE* OF SAN POLO

## L'Arlecchino

**Ruga Rialto, 1729 and 789** (*vaporetto* 1,
S. Silvestro)
☎ 041 716 591
**Every day exc. Sun.**
9.30am-7.30pm.

One of the best selections of leather masks in Venice. Also more affordable papier mâché masks (from L30,000), costumes and loads of souvenirs are on sale here.

## Balocoloc

**Calle Lonea, S. Croce,**
(*vaporetto* 1, S. Stae-B2)
☎ 041 524 05 51
**Every day exc. Mon.**
10.30am-7pm.

If you're looking for the costume that'll make you a star of the Carnival, Balocoloc is a must. Great clothes, masks and cocked hats at reasonable prices.

### *SESTIERE* OF SAN MARCO

## Max Art Shop

**Frezzeria, 1232** (*vaporetti* 1 and 82, San Marco-B2)
☎ 041 523 38 51
❻ 041 528 75 43
**Every day exc. Sun.**
10am-7.30pm.

This shop is the meeting-place of some of the best artist-craftsmen in the city. You'll find a wide variety of masks, marionnettes, collector's dolls, costumes and a multitude of art objects inspired by Venetian traditions. With a little luck, you'll be guided and advised by Antonia Sautter, who founded this Aladdin's Cave.

### THE PRICE OF MASKS

Masks can be made of papier mâché, leather or sometimes even plastic. Prices start at L10,000 (for a white mask) and rise according to the

work involved in making the mask. A leather mask is worth more if it's made of one piece (look on the back).

**A word of advice**
It's better to buy from craftsmen displaying *artigiano veneziano* stickers in their windows, as they make the masks from start to finish. Ordinary shops either buy in white masks that are then painted by workers or simply sell masks bought in batches. Taking into account the intermediaries involved and the profit margins of the shops, you may find you'll pay more for a good mask if you buy in ordinary shops than if you buy from craftsmen. And on top of all this, you may end up with a mass-produced mask. All the mask makers listed here are true craftsmen.

# ANTIQUE HUNTING IN THE SERENISSIMA

## THE MAIN VENETIAN DEALERS

Y̶ou won't have any problem finding the main antique dealers – they're all concentrated around La Fenice and Campo S. M. del Giglio. The problem will be affording something. The Baroque gilded wooden frames, antique furniture, Rococo painted panels and 19th-century paintings are all highly desirable, but cost billions of lire. Only the books and traditional glasses decorated with a gold line won't make too much of a dent in your bank account. And even then, it all depends on their age.

### SESTIERE OF SAN MARCO

### Fabris Giulia Antichità

Campo S. Maurizio, 2606 (*vaporetto* 1, S. M. del Giglio-B2)
☎ 041 523 70 54
Every day exc. Sun. 10am-12.30pm, 3.30-7.30pm.

An interesting antique dealer in Campo S. Maurizio who searches the attics of Venetian residences to find rare items of furniture and old objects. It's easy to imagine the marvels he finds there. The stock often changes so it's worth popping in regularly if you can.

### « M » Antichità

Frezzeria, 1691 (*vaporetto* 1, S. Marco-B/C2)
☎ 041 523 56 66
Every day. exc. Sun. and Mon. morn. 10am-12.30pm, 4-7.30pm.

Here fabulous painted furniture stands alongside antique tableware, the most ornate Venetian mirrors and wooden sculptures from the Baroque age. Opulent and impressive, but not within everyone's means.

### Francisco Saverio Mirate

Calle della Verona, 1904 (*vaporetto* 1, S. M. del Giglio-B2) ☎ 041 522 76 00
Every day exc. Sun. 10am-1pm, 4-8pm.

Another antique shop for you to feast your eyes on, housed in an old Venetian residence, itself worth going out of your way to see. Paintings in gilded period frames (mainly 19th-century), elaborately shaped mirrors and painted wooden furniture, sometimes decorated with trompe-l'œil motifs.

## Beppe Patitucci

**Campo S. M. del Giglio,
2511/B (*vaporetto* 1,
S. M. del Giglio-B2)
☎ 041 523 63 93
Every day exc. Sun.
10am-12.30pm, 4-7.30pm.**

Apart from millionaires, only those fond of old books will have any hope of buying anything in Beppe Patitucci's very smart shop. The rest will look with envy at the magnificent gilded wood furniture and doors painted with Rococo motifs.

## Gian Paolo Tolotti

**Calle del Forno, 42/48
Cannaregio, (*vaporetto* 1,
Ca' d'Oro-B2)
☎ 041 528 52 62
Every day exc. Sun.
9.30am-12.30pm, 4-7.30pm.**

One of the major names in top-quality antiques, with a vast choice of beautiful objects on offer, including old prints, lamp bases, lanterns and small silver objects. These are more affordable, but they can still cost up to a million lire.

## Guiditta I Zancope

**Campo S. Maurizio, 2674
(*vaporetto* 1,
S. M. del Giglio-B2)
☎ 041 523 45 67
Every day exc. Sun. and
Mon. morn. 10am-1pm,
4-7.30pm.**

The house of Guiditta I Zancope has been outwitting all its competitors since 1838. Among the items on display in the shop are old paintings, 19th-century prints, telescopes, retorts and, above all, an incomparable choice of 16th- to 18th-century Venetian glasses, the speciality of this top-quality shop.

## Antichità Zanutto

**Calle delle Veste, 2013
S. Marco (*vaporetto* 1,
S. M. del Giglio-B2)
☎ 041 523 53 59
Every day exc. Sun. 10.30am-
12.30pm, 3.30-7.30pm.**

A marvellous collection of very high-class antiques, including magnificent vases, antique dishes, paintings and

a few pieces of 19th-century furniture. You can also try the

**Campo S. Maurizio second-
hand market**
(see p. 43) and
the shop of **Michele
Cigogna** (see p. 57).

(see p. 43) and the shop of **Michele Cigogna** (see p. 57).

## THE SECOND-HAND MARKETS

Some say there are no longer bargains to be had at the Campo S. Maurizio second-hand market (see p. 43). If you're really mad about antiques, go to the far less well-known market in Jesolo (*vaporetto* 14 to Punta Sabbioni, then a taxi) in July and August. There's also another interesting market in Corso del Popolo in Mestre (frequent trains from Lucia station) the first weekend in every month (except July and August). Be vigilant at all times wherever you are – tourists are considered easy prey here. Bargain hard and read carefully the few basic 'rules' for telling the real from the fake before buying anything (see pp. 28–29).

### How to recognise pure gold gilding

The experts touch the gilding with a rod dipped in nitric acid. If it remains bright at the point of contact, it's pure gold. If it turns black, it's a mixture of gold and copper.

# MURANO GLASSWARE

## GLASS OF EVERY COLOUR

Murano glass comes in all shapes and sizes. To avoid pitfalls in an area that requires an informed eye, first study the real thing at the Murano museum (see p. 66). Then discover some of the secrets of the master glass-makers by visiting one of the island's many workshops or *fornace* (furnaces). If you haven't time for all this, go to the showrooms in Piazza San Marco and the surrounding area, or buy direct from the places listed below, where you'll find the best glass of its kind.

### SESTIERE OF SAN MARCO

#### Battiston

Calle Vallaresso, 1320 (*vaporetto* 1, S. Marco-B2)
☎ 041 523 05 09
Every day 10am-7pm.

One of the main places to buy Murano glass in Venice. There are very beautiful blue glass dishes, pretty coloured bottles that are more affordable (around L100,000 according to size) and, lastly, the well-known carafes of Harry's Bar (just next door) that will look very chic on your table at home.

#### Pauly

Ponte dei Consorsi, 73 (*vaporetti* 1, 52 and 82, S. Zaccaria-C2)
☎ 041 520 98 99
Every day 10am-1pm, 3-7.30pm in season.

In the sumptuous Palazzo Trevisan, a stone's throw from Piazza San Marco, you'll see antique chandeliers and mirrors and 1930s vases, as well as very graceful engraved glasses and dinner services. Fabulous examples of the glass-makers art in a superb setting.

### Venini

Piazzetta dei Leoncini, 314 (*vaporetto* 1, S. Zaccaria-B2)
☎ 041 522 40 45
Every day exc. Sun. and Mon. morn. 10am-1pm, 3-7.30pm.

A famous shop and one of the ten that count around Piazza San Marco. It's a good idea to come to Venini before buying a piece of Murano glassware – it'll give you a pretty good idea of what the best contemporary designers are producing.

### ISLAND OF MURANO
(*vaporetti* 12 and 13 from Fondamente Nuove, 52 from S. Zaccaria-off map)

#### Berengo Fine Arts

Fontamenta Manin, 1
☎ 041 52 74 685
Every day 9.30am-6.30pm.

Dottore Adriano Berengo, who also has a gallery in Arnhem in the Netherlands, had a stroke of genius the day he came up with

## The great names of Murano glass

**Barovier and Toso**:
Fondamenta Vetrai, 28 Murano
☎ 041 73 90 49. Exc. Sun.

**Gino Cenedese**:
Piazza S. Marco, 40
☎ 041 522 54 87.
And also **Mazzega**
(see p. 67).

the idea of asking well-known painters to use Murano glass as their material and to present their works to the public. They make a good, if unusual, investment.

## Domus Vetri d'Arte
**Fondamenta Vetrai, 82**
☎ and ✆ **041 73 92 15**
**Every day 9am-5pm.**

A shop very different from the stalls strung the length of the *fondamente* of Murano. The ashtray/dish may cost L150,000, but it's by Ercole Moretti, one of the best designers around. The warm welcome and personal service come as a bonus.

## Rossi Anna
**Fondamenta Vetrai, 72**
**(*vaporetto* 42, Colonna)**
☎ **041 73 69 45**
**Every day 9am-7pm.**

If you fancy a Murano glass souvenir that's neither bulky nor expensive, then this is the shop for you. You'll find a vast choice of jewellery, bottles and small glass animals (for only L9,000) and other bits and pieces. And, unusually, you can look around without being pestered by a sales assistant.

**Carlo Moretti**:
Fondamenta Manin, 3/13 Murano
☎ 041 73 92 17.

**Archimede Seguso**:
Piazza S. Marco, 61
☎ 041 73 90 48.

### QUICK GUIDE TO GLASS SHOPS

The least expensive articles you can buy in Venice are glass sweets. They're sold for L5,000 in Piazza S. Marco, compared with only L3,000 in Murano. As more expensive objects may also vary greatly in price, the best advice we can give is never to buy in the first shop you come across, unless you really fall in love with something, of course. Another precaution is to examine the glass carefully on all sides. Some 'Murano' glass turns out to be a mere copy from south-east Asia. Be extra careful if the price is low and feel its weight in your hand – good Murano glass must be heavy and should sound like crystal does when you flick it with a finger nail.

Lastly, the glass shops, especially those on Murano, have very flexible opening hours. In summer and during the Carnival, most are open on Sunday and until late at night.

# EATING AND DRINKING

## *DA MANGIARE E DA BERE*

Beware of Venetian grocers – they may turn out to be your downfall. From the side of the *calle*, they'll offer you a multitude of tempting, inexpensive specialities – pasta of every colour, fragrant oil and vinegar, good, strong coffee, bottles of *Prosecco* and aperitifs, and the San Daniele ham that's said to be tastier than that of neighbouring Parma. But beware, all these *etti* (1 *etto* = 100gm/$3\frac{1}{2}$oz) and bottles may add a lot of extra weight to your luggage.

## PASTA OF EVERY COLOUR

### Pastificio Giacomo Rizzo

Salizzada S. Giovanni Crisostomo, 5578 Cannaregio (*vaporetti* 1 and 82, Rialto-B2)
☎ 041 522 28 24
Every day exc. Sun. and Wed. afternoon
8.30am-1pm, 3.30-7.30pm.

Traditional hand-made pasta made with garlic or curry, as well as blue curaçao, dark chocolate and bilberries, but definitely no added colourings. Also *miele amaro di corbezzolo* (bitter arbutus honey) and an amazing variety of olive oils and vinegars (with garlic, basil, lemon, chillies, etc.). But watch out, they cost a fortune.

## HAMS AND CHEESES

### Latteria De Grandis and Sinigaglia

Calle del Mondo Nuovo, 5793/A Castello (*vaporetti* 1 and 82, Rialto-B2)
☎ 041 522 80 62
Every day exc. Sun. and Wed. afternoon
7.30am-1pm, 4.30-7.30pm.

Probably the best choice of hams, sausages and cheeses in the city (and all from Venetia). A handy place to buy San Daniele ham at a very reasonable price.

## WINE, SPIRITS AND COFFEE

### Bottiglieria Colonna

Calle della Fava, 5595 Castello (*vaporetti* 1 and 82, Rialto-B2)
☎ and 🖷 041 528 51 37
Every day exc. Sun.
9am-1pm, 4-8pm.

## WHERE TO FIND GROCER'S SHOPS

Forget the area around Piazza S. Marco and S. Lucia station, where the grocers fleece foreigners without even a smile. Shop where the Venetians shop, on the other side of the Rialto, in Cannaregio (Strada Nova and Rio Terrà S. Leonardo) or Castello (Via G. Garibaldi and around Campo S. M. della Fava). There are also the

**Standa** shops (open every day exc. Sun. 8.30am-7.20pm), the local supermarkets, in Campo S. Luca (S. Marco) or, better still, Strada Nova, near Campo S. Felice.

A wine shop that sells tasting packs containing from three up to a dozen different vintages from Venetia or Lombardy, all for the price of Beaujolais Nouveau, or little more. Ideal for training the palate and getting to know all the varieties of prosecco. Also a wide choice of Italian aperitif wines.

## Casa della Grappa

**Ruga Vecchia, 779/A S. Polo (*vaporetto* 1, Rialto or S. Silvestro-B2)**
☎ **041 523 65 78**
**Every day 8.30am-7.30pm.**

This is the home of grappa. You'll find it here in all its forms (Prosecco grappa, Valpolicella grappa, etc.), and the narrower the bottle, the higher the price (from around L15,000) – not that the shape of the bottle matters. Also a lot of wines and a few cheeses.

## Luciano Mascari

**Ruga degli Speziali, 380 S. Polo (*vaporetti* 1 and 82, Rialto-B2)**
☎ **041 522 97 62**
**Every day exc. Sun. 8am-1pm, 4-7.30pm.**

As well as coffees with heady aromas, one of the best coffee merchants in Venice offers a ridiculous choice of inexpensive herb teas and sweets. The *gianduja* (hazelnut cream with chocolate) in a jar (L8,000) is enough to make you swoon with happiness.

Also the wine merchant **Cantina ai Mori** (see p. 63).

## Rialto market

**Rialto (*vaporetti* 1 and 82, Rialto-B2), market every day exc. Sun. and Mon. (fish market only) 8am-noon. See also pp. 54-55.**

Come here on Saturday from 11am to midday, when it's in full swing. A few places to look out for are the delicatessen at no. 214, the cheesemonger, Sbrissa, at nos. 88-90 and the fresh pasta shop at no. 219 (five or six different sorts of *gnocchi*). Between purchases, go and have a drink at the tiny café at no. 101 (Ruga degli Orefici), opposite the church.

# SWEET SURPRISES

## PANETTERIE AND PASTICCERIE

Very few shops sell both bread and cakes in Venice. It's probably because they attach so much importance to both of them that the Italians prefer to keep them separate. They go to shops specialising in either one or the other – *panetterie* (baker's shops) or *pasticcerie* (patisseries). Do as they do, and go to the big names in Venetian bread or the magicians of tiramisù. It's an experience you'll always remember.

## SESTIERE OF SAN MARCO

### Marchini

Ponte S. Maurizio, 2769
(*vaporetto* 1, Accademia,
S. M. Giglio-A2)
☎ 041 522 91 09
📠 041 528 75 07
Every day exc. Tue.
8.30am-8.30pm.

The best cakes in Venice according to those in the know, and a staggering range to choose from. You have to order the *morellina*, an unforgettable chocolate cake, two days in advance. Try the *barchette*, strawberry tartlets with cream – they're quite delicious.

### Rosa Salva

Campo San Luca, 4589
S. Marco (*vaporetti* 1 and
82, Rialto-B2)
☎ 041 522 53 85
Every day exc. Sun.
7.30am-8.30pm.

This café-pâtisserie is a good place to stop and rest in the city centre. Great choice of sandwiches and

scrumptious hot *fritelle* (Carnival currant doughnuts). Delicious traditional ice cream.

## SESTIERE OF SANTA CROCE

### Gilda Vio

Fondamenta Rio Marin, 890
(*vaporetto* 1, Riva di Biasio-B2)
☎ 041 71 85 23
Every day exc. Wed.
7am-8pm.

One of the best patisseries in Venice can be found in a forgotten district, on the banks of the Rio Marin. The bakery is opposite the shop and you can watch some of Gilda Vio's delicious concoctions being made, including *crostata di marroni* (a chestnut sweet) and, above all, the unforgettable tiramisù.

## SESTIERE OF DORSODURO

### Premiata Pasticceria Tonolo

S. Pantalon, 3764 (*vaporetti* 1 and 82, S. Tomà-A2)
☎ 041 523 72 09
Every day exc. Mon.
7am-7pm.

Since 1886, this has been *the* traditional patisserie of Dorsoduro. A delicious smell of chocolate and vanilla wafts from the bakery next door. In the morning, you can have a frothy cappuccino at the counter. And, if your visit coincides with the Carnival, then come and try the *fritelle*.

## SESTIERE OF CANNAREGIO

### Bruscagrin Il Fornaio

**Strada Nova, 3845**
**(*vaporetto* 1, Ca' d'Oro-B1)**
**☎ 041 522 29 68**
**Every day exc. Sun. 7am-8pm.**

This local bakery makes an incredible variety of bread (with oregano, *pizzaiola*, etc.), as well as the most heavenly cakes. Besides the traditional *fritelle con crema* (cream doughnuts) and *pan del Doge* (bread with almonds and candied fruit), try the *moretto*, a delicious almond and chocolate sweet.

### Martini Fratelli

**Strada Nova, 4310**
**(*vaporetto* 1, Ca' d'Oro-B1)**
**☎ 041 522 72 87**
**Every day exc. Tue. 7am-9pm.**

An unassuming café-patisserie in a district full of tempting sweets. The ones to try here are the Carnival *fritelle*, which are stamped *alla veneziana* (meaning 'made only with currants'). Children will clamour for *baute* (brightly coloured chocolates), which are sold for a very reasonable price (L5,000 per 100gm/3¹/₂oz).

### Pitteri

**Strada Nova, 3843**
**(*vaporetto* 1, Ca' d'Oro-B1)**
**☎ 041 522 26 87**
**Every day 7am-9pm.**

The *zaletti veneziani* or *con pistacchi* (pistachio-flavoured rolls) are so delicious here you don't need to be hungry to eat them, and you can have a cappuccino at the same time. The *baute*, the brightly coloured chocolates you find all over Venice before the Carnival, are very good value for money, too.

## ISLAND OF BURANO

### Costantini

**S. M. SX, 282 Burano**
**(*vaporetti* 12 and 14,**
**Burano-off map)**
**☎ 041 735 595**
**Every day 7am-1pm, 3.30-**
**8pm.**

This unassuming baker's shop is tucked away close to Piazza B. Galuppi. Here you'll find the great cake speciality of the island, *esse buranello*, an S-shaped biscuit that goes very well with tea.

## PANETTERIE AND PASTICCERIE

If you haven't time to go to one of the places recommended in these pages but still want to bring back an *etto* (100gm/3¹/₂oz) of olive bread or Venetian *tiramisù* for your friends, go straight to eat Strada Nova (*sestiere* of Cannaregio), where most *panetterie* and *pasticcerie* are found, sometimes actually next door to each other. The other good place to try is the *sestiere* of S. Polo, between the Rialto and Campo S. Polo. Lastly, the best way to ensure buying quality produce is to look out for the *produzione propria* label that you'll sometimes see on the front of shops. It's a sign that the bread and cakes inside were made on the premises.

# EVERYTHING FOR THE HOME

## TABLEWARE, LINEN AND LACE

Once again, Venice won't fail to amaze you. Its shops offer all kinds of tempting articles, from colourful ceramics to original kitchen utensils, not forgetting the main Venetian speciality, *merletti*, the lace once made by the women of Burano while their fisherman husbands were away at sea. You may still see some of the women today on the thresholds of their brightly coloured houses, making the intricate lace used to decorate tablecloths, napkins and blouses.

### ISLAND OF BURANO

(off map–*vaporetti* 12 from Fondamente Nuove and 14 from S. Zaccaria.)

#### L'Antica Scuola Merletti

Via B. Galuppi, 283
☎ 041 73 54 87
**Every day in season
10am–5.30pm. Closed in Jan.**

One of the best lace shops in Via B. Galuppi. If you're keen on kitsch, you'll find 1950s blouses here for L150,000, as well as frilly lampshades dating back to your grandmother's time.

#### Emilia

Piazza Galuppi, 205-207
☎ 041 73 52 45
**Every day 9.30am-6.30pm.**

The biggest lace shop on the island, if not the best. It stocks an incomparable selection of

tablecloths and napkins, clothes, handkerchiefs and doilies of all sizes at all prices (from L1,000). The charming assistants will be happy to advise you, and there's also a small museum.

#### Martina, merletti d'Arte

Via S. Mauro, 307 and 337
☎ 041 73 55 23

**Every day 10am-6pm
Closed in Jan.**

Leaving aside the table linen, which is nothing out-of-the-ordinary, take a look at the retro blouses selling for around L150,000. Some of them are wearable – if you like frilly embroidery.

## A FEW TIPS IF YOU'RE THINKING OF BUYING LACE

Pay a visit to the lace museum in Burano to see the best there is in the way of Venetian *merletto*. Then go round the shops on the island keeping a cool head. If the price of a sizeable piece of lace is tempting, you're more than likely to be looking at something made in Taiwan. Before you buy a piece, look it over very carefully and find out where it was made.

## SESTIERE OF SAN MARCO

### Jesurum

**Merceria del Capitello, 4857
(*vaporetti* 1, 52 and 82,
S. Marco-B2)
☎ 041 520 61 77
Every day in season
9.30am-1pm, 3-7.30pm.**

You'll find this extraordinary showroom behind the basilica, in the former Scuola S. Apollonia, a veritable monument to the splendour of the large trading companies. Here you can admire or buy not only the finest lace in Venice, but also household linen and ladies' fashions. Here, too, you'll see tables laid with exquisite tableware that will make you truly envious. Jesurum, which is unquestionably the best place to buy table linen and lace, has several other shops in the city, including one in Piazza San Marco, 60-61
☎ 041 522 98 64.
Their prices may be high, but you can find tablecloths that will impress your guests for as little as L200,000

or L300,000 – or even less during the January and July clearance sales.

### Epicentro

**Calle dei Fabbri, 932
(*vaporetti* 1 and 82,
S. Marco-B2)
☎ 041 522 68 64
🖷 041 522 50 87
Every day exc. Sun.
10am-7.30pm.**

If you dream of having ultra-modern Italian ladles, pie slices and other kitchen utensils for your home, then this is the place for you. You can find everything here, from high-tech cheese graters to the latest in fruit bowls. There are also very fine coffeepots and sets to help you recapture all the flavour of Italian coffee when you get home. Italian chic obviously doesn't come cheap in this area but the prices are still affordable.

## SESTIERE OF SANTA CROCE

### Ceramiche

**Sottoportigo della signora Bettina (between Calle della Regina and Campo S. Cassiano-B2), 2345
(*vaporetto* 1, S. Stae-B2)
☎ 041 72 31 20
Every day 10am-7pm.**

Yellow and blue ceramics with floral motifs that will brighten up your table without ruining you. There are two styles of dishes, with prices starting at L45,000 for the smallest. Why pay more when La Bottega ceramics are all hand painted as well?

# VENETIAN FASHION

## CLOTHES AND ACCESSORIES

Venice isn't Milan, the home of Italian fashion, and it's often said that it isn't the best place to buy an Italian outfit. However, this isn't always the case. There are many small shops that don't bump up prices, where you can find original, inexpensive accessories, good-quality jumpers and great suits to wear for a season.

### SESTIERE
### OF SAN MARCO

#### Arabescque-Saldarini & Saldarini

Castello 3403, Ponte dei Greci (*vaporetti* 1 and 52, S. Zaccaria-C2)
☎ 041 522 81 77
Every day exc. Sun. 10am-1pm, 3.30-7.30pm.

Among the many high-quality accessories on sale in this shop, you'll find crumpled silk squares from L120,000,

and masses of elegant scarves and stoles. The sales assistants won't try to rush you because they know it can be difficult to choose.

#### Brocca

Mercerie del Capitello, 4858 (*vaporetti* 1 and 82, Rialto-B2)
☎ 041 522 54 51
Every day 9.30am-1pm, 3-7.30pm.

A tiny shop entirely devoted to men's pullovers of every kind – sporty or casual. You can treat yourself to Italian chic here without spending a fortune (from L100/150,000), and during the sales you can pick up some real bargains.

#### Camiceria San Marco

Calle Vallaresso, 1340 (*vaporetti* 1 and 82, S. Marco-B2)
☎ 041 522 14 32
Every day exc. Sun. and Mon. morn. 9am-1pm, 3-7.30pm.

The leading specialist in shirts and blouses for years, as well as made-to-measure pyjamas in an endless variety of fabrics and colours. Very expensive though.

#### Coin

Salizzada S. Giovanni Crisostomo, B2 5787 Cannaregio
☎ 041 239 80 00
Every day exc. Sun. 9.30am-7.30pm.

*The* department store of Venice, where you can browse in peace and get a good overview of Italian fashion. Two of the floors are devoted to ladies' fashion, one to men's and one to the home.

#### Max & Co

Mercerie S. Salvador, 5028 (*vaporetti* 1 and 82, S. Marco)
☎ 041 523 08 17. Every day exc. Sun. 9.30am-7.30pm.

The young line of the Max Mara group can be found in the heart of Venice's shopping district, but only a tiny part of the collection is displayed in the window. Tucked away inside, you'll find smart outfits for women that are relatively affordable.

## Max Mara

**Merceria dell'Orologio, 268-272 (*vaporetti* 1 and 82, S. Marco-B2) ☎ 041 522 66 88.**

A simple, uncluttered shop window is home to the creations of the great name in top-quality ready-to-wear fashion. The prices are not much less here than outside Italy, but there's far more to choose from, with good bargains to be had in the sales.

## La Perla

**Campo S. Salvador, 4828 (*vaporetti* 1 and 82, Rialto-B2) ☎ 041 522 64 59 Every day exc. Sun. and Mon. morn. 9.30am-12.30pm, 3.30-7.30pm.**

Fancy some chic underwear? Here you'll find the ultimate in Italian lingerie. La Perla's bras and suspender belts are feminine and frilly, and the prices are in line with the fantasies.

## Araba fenice

**S. Marco 1882 (*vaporetti* 1 and 82, S. Marco-B2) ☎ 041 522 06 64. Every day exc. Sun. 9.30am-7.30pm.**

Everything in this sober, elegant shop – the clothes, the jewellery and the decor – was designed by a group of artists who placed the emphasis on materials and forms. Every design is exclusive and the items are virtually unique, with only one made of each size. It's also one of the few places in Italy where the majestic jewellery of the Danish designer, Moonies, can be found. Don't miss it.

## SESTIERE OF CANNAREGIO

## Metropoli

**Salizzada S. Giovanni Crisostomo, 5644 (*vaporetti* 1 and 82, Rialto-B2) ☎ 041 523 62 02 . Every day exc. Sun. in Jul.-Aug. 9.30am-1pm, 3.30-7.30pm.**

THE FAMOUS LABELS

All the big names in Italian haute-couture and ready-to-wear clothes have branches near Piazza S. Marco:

**Prada**: S. Marco, Salizada, S. Moise, 1464-1469 ☎ 041 52 83 966.

**Elysée 1**: Frezzeria, 1693 ☎ 041 522 30 20. Armani and Bagutta lines.

**Fiorellashop**: (see p. 43).

**La Tour**: Calle Larga S. Marco, 287 ☎ 041 522 51 47 Aida Barni lines.

**Et Missoni**: Calle Vallaresso, 1312 ☎ 041 520 57 33.

**Gianni Versace**: Campo S. Moise, S. Marco, 1426 ☎ 041 52 00 057.

**Laura Biagiotti**: Calle Larga XXII Marzo, 2401 ☎ 041 520 34 01. Cl. Sun.

**Valentino**: Salizzada S. Moisè, 1473 ☎ 041 520 57 33.

Middle-of-the-range ready-to-wear clothes. Take a look at the velvet dresses – they're comfortable, pretty and trendy. Metropoli has another outlet in the same street, near the Rialto at the sign of Anni Ruggenti (5579 Cannaregio ☎ 041 523 83 89).

Also see page 115 for a list of places to buy unusual and second-hand clothes.

# LEATHER IN ALL ITS FORMS

No visit to Italy would be complete without the purchase of a pair of chic Italian shoes or a *vero cuoio* (real leather) wallet, belt or handbag. A trip to Venice is no exception. Don't try to fight temptation – it may cost you several hundred thousand lire, but it's an investment you won't regret.

## LEATHER SHOPS

### *SESTIERE* OF SAN MARCO

### La Bottega Veneta

**Calle Vallaresso, 1337 (*vaporetti* 1 and 82, S. Marco-B2)**
☎ **041 520 28 16**
**Every day 10am-7.30pm.**

This *bottega* is an excellent place to find original, elegant handbags and exclusive silk scarves. It specialises in plaited leather for women and is fairly expensive.

### La Coupole

**Calle Larga XXII Marzo, 2366 (*vaporetti* 1 and 82, S. Marco-B2)**
☎ **041 522 42 43**
**Every day 9.30am-6.30pm.**

*The* Venetian leather and suede specialist stocks famous names for

both men and women including Alaïa, Montana, Antonio Fusco, Dolce e Gabbana and V2 by Versace.

### Fendi

**Salizzada S. Moisè, 1474 (*vaporetti* 1 and 82, S. Marco-B2)**
☎ **041 520 57 33**
**Every day 10am-7.30pm.**

A high-class Italian leather shop for women with a variety of chic, elegant creations (clothes, luggage, etc.) on display in the window. The Fendi label doesn't come cheap, but it's one you can rely on.

### Marforio

**Mercerie S. Salvador, 5033 (*vaporetti* 1 and 82, Rialto-B2)**
☎ **041 522 57 34**
**Every day exc. Sun. 9am-12.30pm, 3-7.30pm.**

It's difficult not to be tempted by such an array of belts, luggage and wallets, all in the best possible taste and bearing names such as Valentino, Bridge-Firenze and Luciano Soprani – in other words, the best in the business. Obviously, not everything here is affordable, far from it, but you can still find a woman's purse for under L100,000. Even if you don't find what you're looking for, the shop alone is well worth seeing.

## Vogini

**Calle Larga XXII Marzo,
1301/1305
(*vaporetti* 1 and 82,
S. Marco-B2)
☎ 041 528 79 33
Every day exc. Sun.
9am-7.30pm.**

Probably the best leather
shop in Venice. You must
see it for its incomparable
choice of handbags, as
well as the clothes, luggage
and accessories for men.
Everything's expensive,
but good value for money
in the end.

## SHOE SHOPS

### *SESTIERE*
OF SAN MARCO

#### Bruno Magli

**Calle Vallaresso, 1302
(*vaporetti* 1 and 82,
S. Marco-B2)
☎ 041 522 72 10
Every day 10am-7.30pm.**

Anyone who likes traditional
shoes should pay a visit to
this shop, especially if they're
men. The women's shoes,
though elegant, are
unadventurous. Prices start
at around L300,000.

#### Bata

**Merceria S. Zulian,
4979/A-4982, S. Marco-B2
(*vaporetti* 1 and 82,
S. Marco)
☎ 041 522 97 66
Every day 9.30am-7.30pm.**

If you've come across Bata
before, you may be in for
a surprise. You'll find masses
of choice and unbeatable
prices (starting at under

L100,000 for a pair of men's
shoes). It's a good place to
come before heading for the
big shoe shops.

### *SESTIERE*
OF CANNAREGIO

#### Mori & Bozzi

**Strada Nova, 2367-A
(*vaporetto* 1, Ca' d'Oro-A2)
☎ 041 71 52 61
Every day 9.30am-12.30pm,
1.30-7.30pm.**

A good place to buy Italian
footwear, with young designs
and all the latest fashions,
especially for women, at very
reasonable prices.

#### Atelier Rolando
Segalin, il calzolaio
di Venezia

**Calle delle Fuseri, 4365
S. Marco (*vaporetti* 1 and
82, Rialto or S. Marco-B2)
☎ 041 522 21 15
Every day exc. Sat. afternoon
and Sun. 9am-noon,
3.30-7.30pm.**

This is a place that dreams
are made of and out of the
reach of most. Segalin
makes shoes to measure
to suit your whim (you
can have them sent
home) whether they
are in lizardskin
or ostrich, or the
strangest of
shapes. It's a
shop you
really
mustn't
miss.

## QUICK GUIDE TO ITALIAN SHOES

Quality, strength, good
looks, a variety of
styles and amazing colours
(for women) all make
buying Italian shoes a
sure bet. Nothing could be
easier, either. The sales
assistants are quite accustomed
to foreigners. If your stay
coincides with the sales,
make a point of going
down Calle Larga XXII
Marzo or the Mercerie,
where most of the shoe
shops are located.

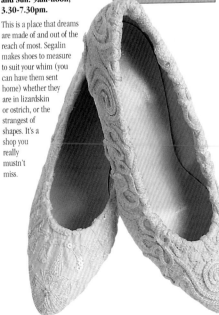

# ALL THAT GLITTERS

## JEWELLERY SHOPS AND WORKSHOPS

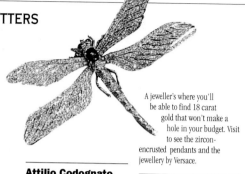

The Venetian goldsmiths have carved themselves an excellent reputation. All their creations are dazzlingly beautiful, but even the least costs an arm and a leg. If you can't hope to acquire one of these treasures, try looking in side streets instead. The Murano glass jewellery you can buy there – bracelets and necklaces – will make equally good souvenirs of the city.

### SESTIERE OF SAN MARCO

### Bucintoro Arte

Merceria del Capitello, 4924 (*vaporetti* 1 and 82, Rialto-B2)
☎ and **F** 041 523 01 31
Every day exc. Sun.
9.30am-7.30pm.

A dealer specialising in antique jewellery, whose shop you definitely should see if you're interested in buying some. His prices are only slightly higher than those of Attilio Codognato, his main competitor.

A jeweller's where you'll be able to find 18 carat gold that won't make a hole in your budget. Visit to see the zircon-encrusted pendants and the jewellery by Versace.

### Attilio Codognato

Calle dell'Ascensione, 1295 (*vaporetti* 1 and 82, S. Marco-B2)
☎ 041 522 50 42
Every day exc. Sun. and Mon. 10am-1pm, 4-7pm.

If you only like antique jewellery, then this pretty shop is for you. You'll find here the widest possible choice of rings, as well as cameos and a few contemporary pieces, but they're all very expensive.

### Chimento

Campo S. Moisè, 1460, S. Marco (*vaporetti* 1 and 82, S. M. del Giglio-B2)
☎ 041 523 60 10
Every day exc. Sun. and Mon. morn. Nov.-Mar. 9.30am-7pm.

### Herriz

Calle Larga XXII Marzo, 2381 (*vaporetti* 1 and 82, S. Marco-B2)
☎ 041 520 42 76
Every day exc. Sun. and Mon. 10am-7pm.

This renowned antique shop sells a vast range of antique jewellery made by famous names. Splashing out here will be a real investment.

### Missiaglia

Piazza S. Marco 125 (*vaporetti* 1 and 82, S. Marco-B2)
☎ 041 522 44 64
Every day exc. Sun. 9.30am-12.30pm, 3.30-7.30pm.

A must – Missiaglia is none other than the appointed supplier to the great Venetian and Italian families since 1846. You really should go along to this jeweller's and goldsmith's (at least to look in the window) where you'll find objects to rival those of any other great city. Some exclusive items (lighters and necklaces in particular) are the work of highly talented Venetian artists. Next to the café Quadri.

## Nardi

**Piazza S. Marco, 69
(*vaporetti* 1 and 82,
S. Marco-B2)
☎ 041 523 21 50
Every day exc. Sun. and Mon.
morn. 9.30am-1pm, 3-7.30pm.**

This is the other great jeweller's of Piazza San Marco besides Missiaglia. Among other pieces of jewellery, Nardi has created an Othello brooch encrusted with precious stones. You can also admire the elaborate work on the more affordable clocks, boxes, frames and compacts. Next to the café Florian.

## Passoni

**S. Polo, 64 (*vaporetti* 1
and 82, Rialto-B2)
☎ 041 522 55 19
Every day exc. Sun. and Mon.
morn. 9.30am-12.30pm,
3.30-7.30pm.**

One of the best jewellery shops in the *Mercerie*. It sells classically elegant designs and some rings are even affordable (for Venice).

## SESTIERE OF SAN POLO

## Sfriso

**Campo S. Tomà, 2849
(*vaporetti* 1 and 82,
S. Tomà-A2)
☎ 041 522 35 58
Every day exc. Sun.
9am-12.30pm, 3.30-7pm.**

At Sfriso, every piece is unique and hand-crafted with the tools of another age. The intimidating little shop in Campo S. Tomà houses all sorts of objects (ewers, dishes, cups, compacts, boxes and so on) made of gold or, more often, silver. The prices are astronomical, of course, but the name Sfriso is well-respected.

## THE JEWELLERS OF THE RIALTO

When a piece of jewellery is affordable here, it means it's made of a mere 18 carat gold. Take your time and compare prices before buying. The shopkeepers of the Rialto have a tendency to take advantage of tourists.

### Costume jewellery

This inexpensive jewellery is often made of colourful Murano glass. You'll find plenty of rings but even more bracelets

and necklaces in most of the glass shops on the island (see pp. 96–97). If you're looking for somewhere in Venice itself, you could try:

### Totem-Il Canale

Rio Terrà A. Foscarini, 878-B (*vaporetti* 1 and 82, Accademia) ☎ 041 522 36 41. Every day exc. Sun. 10am-1pm, 3-7pm. This African art gallery reserves a little space for *antiche perle veneziane* (antique Venetian pearl) jewellery. Prices start at L30,000 for a bracelet.

# CHILDREN'S VENICE

## CLOTHES, TOYS AND GAMES

As you stroll through Venice, you should be able to find presents for your children without too much difficulty. If they aren't very interested in clothes, you can always fall back on the turned wooden toys made by craftsmen, model gondolas, or small brightly coloured Murano glass objects which they can show off to their friends.

### SESTIERE OF SAN MARCO

## Chicco Guardaroba

Mercerie dell'Orologio, 217 (*vaporetti* 1 and 82, S. Marco-B2) ☎ 041 522 94 32 🅕 041 522 55 41 Every day 9.30am-7.30pm, Sun. 10am-7pm.

You'll find '*Tutto per il bambino*' here, as the publicity blurb says. The shop is entirely devoted to children's clothes and is a great place to give your offspring an Italian look for around L70,000.

## F.G.B.

Campo S. M. del Giglio, 2459 (*vaporetto* 1, S. M. del Giglio-B2) ☎ and 🅕 041 523 65 56 Every day 10am

You'll find things to interest young and old alike at Giorgio Bubacco's shop. You can buy original masks here, as well as good, inexpensive costume jewellery and lifesize Murano glass insects that children love (including a wasp for L10,000, a ladybird for L12,000, a scorpion and other creepy-crawlies).

### SESTIERE OF DORSODURO

## Emporio Pettenello SAS

Campo S. Margherita, 2978 (A2) ☎ 041 523 11 67 Every day exc. Sun. (open during the Carnival) 9.30am-1pm, 3.30-8pm.

An Aladdin's cave that will bring back childhood memories. You'll find all kinds of toys at all kinds of prices for your offspring, from kaleidoscopes to adorable musical boxes, mobiles, pretty dolls and small reproductions of various objects (including *forcole*, gondola oar rests, and *brocole*, lagoon poles). You'll always be welcomed with a smile.

## SESTIERE OF SAN POLO

### Albero

**S. Polo, 2312**
**(*vaporetti* 1, S. Tomà-A2)**
**☎ 041 710 248**
**Every day exc. Sun.**
**10am-1pm, 4-7.30pm.**

From the flowers to the pencil-holder tree (L30,000) or the souvenir key ring (L10,000), there's a whole world of wooden toys and small objects here that should delight your children. And you, too, no doubt. If you want a chess set or something similar, then consider it made. They'll write you out an invoice and once made send the goods to your home.

### Dalla Venezia-Angelo

**Calle dello Scaletèr, 2204**
**(*vaporetto* 1, S. Tomà-A2)**
**☎ 041 72 16 59**
**Open**
**irregularly**
**(phone in**
**advance).**

This is another good place to find unusual and original toys. Wood is king here and, with a little luck, you'll see the craftsman at work in his shop. The pretty tops would make good presents – they don't cost much and they're easy to pack.

## SESTIERE OF CASTELLO

### Protagonisti

**Salizzada S. Lio, 5792**
**(*vaporetti* 1 and 82, Rialto-B2)**
**☎ 041 523 58 97**
**Every day exc. Sun. 9.30am-12.30pm, 4-7.30pm.**

Definitely the best place in Venice to dress your children (0–15 years) from head to toe, in bright colours and all the latest fashions. The delightful outfits for girls (under L.100,000) will make their friends green with envy.

### MORE GIFT IDEAS

If you've given up hope of finding presents for your children, you needn't go home empty-handed. You can always fall back on Carnival objects (see pp. 92–93), the card games sold by some *legatorie* (see pp. 88–89) or sweets. Pots of *gianduja* (see p. 99), colourful chocolates and cakes (see pp. 100–101) should all go down well. Or why not try something kitsch? Then there are all the knick-knacks in the tourist shops around Piazza San Marco. Gondolier's hats and winking gondolas may do the trick, not to mention the pretty plastic balls containing snowscenes of the basilica.

### La Scialuppa

**Calle II° Saoneri, 2681**
**(*vaporetti* 1 and 82,**
**S. Tomà-A2)**
**☎ 041 719 372**
**Every day exc. Sun.**
**9am-6pm (open irregularly).**

A tiny shop devoted to the sea and all that sails on it. There are models of old boats to put together and, best of all, gondola kits for around L35,000 with detailed assembly instructions. They'll please young and old alike.

# READING AND RELAXING

## BOOKS, PRINTS AND RECORDS

I f you like fine books or reproductions of old prints, you won't be disappointed. Venice has a large number of bookshops whose shelves are literally collapsing under the weight of art books, sometimes at bargain prices. Many also publish works on unusual subjects that are part of Venetian culture. Where records are concerned, Venice can be a little disappointing as there are only a handful of music shops in the city. More's the pity, since CDs sell for a good price in Italy.

## SESTIERE OF SAN MARCO

### Libreria Bertoni

Calle de la Mandola, 3637-B
(*vaporetto* 1, S. Angelo-B2)
☎ 041 522 95 83
Every day exc. Sun. and Aug.
9am-12.30pm, 3.30-7.30pm.

A family run bookshop that's been handed down from father to son. It has new, old and second-hand books on art and architecture. You have to rummage around, but you can usually find something of interest.

### Fantoni Libri

Salizzada S. Luca, 4119
(*vaporetti* 1 and 82,
Rialto-B2)
☎ 041 522 07 00
Every day exc. Sun.
9am-12.30pm, 3.30-7.30pm.

A bookshop you shouldn't miss if you like fine books and art books or are interested in architecture and design. It also has a selection of reviews that will fascinate fans of architecture and the graphic arts.

### Libreria Goldoni

Calle dei Fabbri, 4742
(*vaporetti* 1 and 82,
Rialto-B2)
☎ 041 522 23 84
Every day exc. Sun.
9.30am-7.30pm.

An excellent general bookshop with a fine choice of guides. For a fairly tidy sum, you

can buy a facsimile that will make your friends green with envy – nine long plates of all the houses on the Grand Canal. It's a faithful reproduction of the 1828 work owned by the Biblioteca Marciana.

### Sansovino

Bacino Orseolo, 84
(*vaporetti* 1 and 82,
S. Marco-B2)
☎ 041 522 26 23
Every day 9am-7.30pm in season.

If you're looking for a detailed plan of the city, a guide, or a book about a great Venetian painter, it's here that you'll find it. Situated

## A RECORD SHOP

### Nalesso

**Calle Spezièr, 2765/D
S. Marco (*vaporetto* 1,
S. M. del Giglio-B2)
☎ 041 520 33 29
Every day 9.30am-
12.30pm, 3.30-7.30pm
(Sun. 4-7.30pm).**

Lovers of the Baroque will want to head straight for this record and music shop. It has a wide choice of 17th- and 18th-century Venetian music and you may be lucky to come across that rare find, the productions of the Italian record labels *Tactus, Nuova Era, Sinfonia* and *Dynamic*, which can be difficult to find elsewhere. Music lovers can also buy *Venezia, i luoghi della musica (The Musical Places in Venice)* at this shop. It's a guide listing all the churches and palaces connected with the great musicians, from Monteverdi and Cavalli to Vivaldi and Wagner.

near the *bacino*, which is peopled with gondoliers, it is located in one of the most photogenic places in Venice.

## SESTIERE OF DORSODURO

### Toletta

**Sacca della Toletta, 1214
(*vaporetti* 1 and 82, Ca' Rezzonico Accademia-A2)
☎ 041 523 20 34
Every day exc. Sun.
9am-12.45pm, 3.30-7.30pm.**

*The* place in Venice to buy new and second-hand art books at reduced prices (up to 50% off). According to those in the know,

there's nowhere else like it in Italy. Another place you can try (no shop sign) is Rio Terrà Degli Assassini, 3637-B S. Marco (*vaporetto* 1, S. M. del Giglio), every day. except Sun. 9am-12.30pm, 3-7.30pm. You'll find pile upon pile of new art books and fine books at unbeatable prices. You have to rummage around.

## SESTIERE OF CASTELLO

### Filippi

**Calle del Paradiso, 5763
(*vaporetti* 1 and 82,
Rialto-B2)
☎ 041 523 56 35
Every day 9am 12.30pm
3.30-7.30pm.**

A publishing house and bookshop without rival for everything to do with the Serenissima. If there's a work (old or new) on any aspect of the history of Venice, you're almost certain to find it here. There are also fine reproductions of old prints at affordable prices.

### Ca' Foscinara 2

**Dorsoduro 3259, 3123
☎ 041 522 9602
Mon.-Fri., 9am-1pm
and 3-7pm.**

This is the bookshop of the Ca' Foscari University and it has the largest collection of books in English to be found in Venice, so come here for a browse if the weather's wet. It sells mainly literature and poetry.

*An old edition of Goldoni at Toletta*

# VENETIAN RARITIES

## SHOPS FOR THOSE WHO LOVE VENICE

If the usual souvenirs leave you cold and make you want to track down a rarity, something truly original that no other tourist will have, then search no more. These pages contain the addresses of true craftsmen, specialising in very different areas. They'll offer you the best in Venice, without necessarily ruining you – gilded frames, marvellous ceramics, antique old clothes and you can even visit a gondola manufacturer.

known in Venice for his artistry. You can see him restoring furniture and gilded wooden frames, especially the fabulous Art Deco designs that he sells for a tidy sum.

## A PRINTER

### Gianni Basso

**Calle del Fumo, 5306
Cannaregio
(*vaporetto* 51,
Fondamente Nuove-C1)
☎ 041 523 46 81
Every day exc. Sat. aft. and
Sun. 9am-12.30pm, 3-7pm.**

The tiny shop and workshop of the *stampatore* (printer) Gianni Basso isn't easy to find. It's a fascinating place with a strong smell of ink where you can choose a logo for your visiting card, like the actor Hugh Grant and others before you. Prices start at L15–20,000.

## A GILDER

### A. Barutti Lacador

**Campo Manin, 4231
S. Marco (*vaporetti* 1 and 82,
S. Angelo or Rialto-B2)
☎ 041 528 73 16
Every day exc. Sun.
9am-12.30pm, 2-7.30pm.**

Alfredo Barutti, in his timeless shop in Campo Manin, is well

## UNUSUAL OBJECTS

### Livio de Marchi

**Salizzada S. Samuele,
3157/A. S. Marco (*vaporetto*
82, S. Samuele-A2)
☎ 041 528 56 94
Every day exc. Sun. 9.30am-
12.30pm, 1.30-6.30pm.**

The only shop and workshop of its kind in Venice, where you can find the amusing designs of Livio de Marchi, including socks, shirts, ties and a variety of other objects made of wood. The prices vary, but there are some affordable bits and pieces to be found.

### Nel Giardino del Tempo

**Fondamenta dei Frari, 2562
S. Polo (*vaporetti* 1 and 82,
S. Tomà-A2)
☎ 041 524 46 42
Every day exc. Sun.
10am-1pm, 3-7.30pm.**

At least take a look in the window of the shop run by this creative young craftswoman and designer. You'll see bookmarks inspired by the work of Marcel Duchamp that sell for the modest sum of L15,000. Unusual and idiosycratic items and a frequently changing window display.

## BASSANO CERAMICS

### Rigattieri

Calle dei Frati, 3532-3536 S. Marco (*vaporetto* 1, S. Angelo-B2) ☎ 041 522 76 23 Every day exc. Sun. and Mon. morn. 9am-1pm, 3-8pm.

The best choice of tableware made in Bassano, a small town in the country specialising in the production of hand-painted ceramics that sell for a correspondingly high price. The shop window full of vases, tureens, eggs and animals is amazing.

## UNUSUAL CLOTHES

### Caterina

Calle de la Botteghe, 3185 Dorsoduro (*vaporetto* 1, Ca' Rezzonico-B2) Every day exc. Sun. and Mon. morn. 10am-12.30pm, 4-7pm.

A great place to buy second-hand clothes in Venice. You'll have to rummage around but, with a little patience, you'll find the dress or hat that will impress your friends – without necessarily spending much, either.

### 869

Calle Nuova Sant'Agnese, 869 Dorsoduro (*vaporetti* 1 and 82, Accademia-A2) ☎ 041 520 60 70 Every day exc. Sun. and Tue. morn. 10.30am-6.30pm.

This is where the famous paintings of Kandinsky, Klee and Magritte are portrayed in dresses and hand-knitted jumpers that sell for a price. You obviously won't need to worry afterwards about causing a sensation when you walk in the *calle!*

## Laboratorio Arte & Costume di Monica Daniele

Sant'Agostin, S. Polo 2199 (*vaporetti* 1 and 82, S. Tomà-A2). ☎ 041 524 62 42 Every day exc. Sun. 10am-12.30pm, 3-6.30pm.

Antique dresses, hats and scarves to parade around in at festivals or for the evening. Rummage about and you'll find what you're looking for at Monica Daniele's, even old dolls. From L20,000 for soft toys to L500,000 for dresses and costumes.

# Nightlife Practicalities

Venice has a vibrant nightlife, involving theatres, concerts and festivals, and people usually stay up late, so make the most of it. Besides meeting-places and lively, friendly bars serving wine or beer (some of which close around midnight or 1pm), there are a handful of discos and a casino to take you through the night.

## HOW TO FIND OUT WHAT'S ON

Once you get there, read the appropriate column in one of the two regional dailies, *La Nuova Venezia* or *Il Gazzettino*, or get a copy of the free monthly publication *Un Ospite di Venezia* (from the tourist information office). This includes details of the main musical and theatrical performances taking place in the city. To find out the dates of the major events of the Venetian calendar, send a fax or write to the *Azienda di Promozione Turistica di Venezia* (Castello, 4421, 30122 Venezia ☎ 041 529 87 11 📠 041 523 03 99), which will send you a brochure listing all the cultural events taking place in the city month by month.

## HOW TO BOOK

Except for operas, for which it's difficult, if not impossible, to get seats without reserving several weeks in advance, getting hold of concert or theatre tickets shouldn't be a problem.

Simply go along to the ticket office (reservations are rarely made by phone), where you will sometimes be asked to pay the *prevendita*, or 10 % of the ticket price. You can also get tickets from travel agents (for a complete list, see *Un Ospite di Venezia*) and, for classical music concerts only, from **Nalesso** (see box on p. 113), the big Venetian classical record shop.

## PRICES

A ticket for the Goldoni, the best theatre in Venice, costs around L40,000, while a ticket for a concert costs in the region of L25,000. The exact price obviously depends on who is performing. It's worth bearing in mind that many concerts are free, especially in churches.

Cinema tickets are approximately the same price as in the UK, i.e. L11,000-15,000 lire (£4-5).

## WHAT TO WEAR

Generally speaking the Venetians dress elegantly. Do as they do and wear something suitable for wherever you'll be spending the evening – casual clothes if you're heading for a bar or something more dressy if you're going to a piano-bar or the theatre.

## THE *PASSEGGIATA*

The traditional *passeggiata*, the Italians' pre-dinner walk, is a ritual observed in Venice and elsewhere throughout the year. Dressed to the nines and eating an ice-cream cornet, you, too, can make your way through the Mercerie from Piazza S. Marco to Campo S. Bartolomeo, the square near the Rialto that's packed with people (especially the young) at around 8pm. The other 'route' takes you from the Rialto to Campo S. Polo, via Ruga Vecchia and Ruga Ravano. It attracts fewer people, but as the *calle* are narrower, it's just as crowded.

## LIVELY PLACES

The Venetians meet up in the *campi*, each of which has its regulars. Campo S. Luca attracts teenagers because of the McDonald's. Campo S. Stefano is more elegant and is a good place to have a *spritz*, the Venetian Campari-based aperitif, before dinner. Last but not least, Campo S. Margherita is the favourite of students and intellectuals. You can have an after-dinner drink in one of the many bars around it.

### THE CANALS BY NIGHT

A boat ride on the Grand Canal at night shouldn't be missed. The most beautiful 'street' in the world is a magical sight. You can see it from the 1 *vaporetto*, which takes you from S. Lucia station to Piazza S. Marco, departing every 10 minutes (every hour from 1 to 4am). You really shouldn't miss a gondola ride along the quieter canals, either.

# MUSIC

## Al Paradiso Perduto

**Fondamenta della
Misericordia, 2540
Cannaregio
(*vaporetti* 1 and 82, S.
Marcuola-B1)
☎ 041 72 05 81
Every day except
Wed. and Aug.
7pm-1am (2am Sat.).**

An authentic *osteria* where you can dine to the sound of jazz. There's live music on Sunday and Monday, and poetry readings on Monday as well. With lots of students in the audience, there's a great atmosphere. Definitely a place to frequent.

## Da Codroma

**Dorsoduro 2540 (*vaporetto*
1, Ca' Rezzonico-A2)
☎ 041 524 67 89
Every day except Sat.
8am-midnight**

This *osteria*, founded 130 years ago, still has its original large walnut tables, wooden chairs and old bar. *Cichèti*, all the sandwiches you could want, and a very good choice of the wines of Venetia and the neighbouring regions. The atmosphere is convivial and you'll get a warm welcome. Live music every Tuesday (jazz, blues, Latin and soul). Highly recommended.

## Round Midnight

**Dorsoduro, Fondamentina
dei Pugni, 3102 (*vaporetto*
1, Ca' Rezzonico-A2)
☎ 041 523 20 56**

**Every day except Sun.
8pm-2am.**

A tiny place with a New York atmosphere a stone's throw from Campo di S. Margherita. You can listen to high-quality music (acid jazz and trip hop) here, as well as dancing the tango or watching a cabaret show. You'll find guides to the shows (*Venezia da Vivere*) in the cafés in the *campo*.

## Fondaco Cini

**S. Giorgio Maggiore,
S. Marco (*vaporetti* 52 and
82, S. Giorgio-C3)
Information and reservations
☎ 041 528 99 00.**

As well as major concerts, there are lectures (in Italian, of course). It's also a unique opportunity to see the Palladian cloisters around which this important foundation has grown up.

## Church of La Pietà

**Riva degli Schiavoni,
Castello (*vaporetti* 1, 10, 52
and 82, S. Zaccaria-B2)
☎ 041 523 10 96
Tickets and reservations at
the church.**

Faithful to the memory of Vivaldi, one of Venice's major musical venues stages a large number of concerts of 18th-century Venetian music, featuring Vivaldi, as well as Albinoni, Galuppi, Marcello and others. Music-lovers will enjoy the acoustics, which can improve otherwise second-rate strings. If any of the best Italian exponents of the genre are performing here – Il Giardino Armonico or Europa Galante in particular – hurry along to get tickets.

## Palazzo Labia

**S. Geremia, Cannaregio 275
(*vaporetti* 1 and 82,
S. Marcuola-B1)
☎ 041 71 66 66.**

Come to the free concerts produced by Rai, the Italian equivalent of the BBC, and take advantage of an unexpected opportunity to see the wonderful ceilings painted by Tiepolo (with guided tours on Wednesdays, Thursdays and Fridays at 3pm and 4pm). ☎ 041524 28 12. It'll be a night to remember, so make sure you don't miss it.

# OTHER PLACES

Venice has a vibrant musical scene, but you have to like classical music because the other kinds are less well catered for. Look at the posters along the calle – with a bit of luck, your stay will coincide with a concert in one of the churches, perhaps in the marvellous setting of Santa Maria dei Frari, San Samuele or the Scuola Grande di San Giovanni Evangelista. As well as the normal programme of events, an interesting international festival of contemporary music takes place (in July in odd years) during the Venice Biennale. For information and programmes, contact Ca' Giustinian, 30124 Venezia ( ☎ 041 521 87 11, ✆ 041 520 05 69.

# THEATRES

## Teatro Carlo Goldoni

S. Marco, 4650/B
(*vaporetti* 1 and 82, Rialto-B2)
☎ 041 520 54 22 and
041 520 75 83
Box office open Mon.-Fri.
10am-1pm, 4.30-7pm.

Probably the most interesting theatre in the city. You may see the plays of Goldoni performed here, as well as contemporary repertory and even musicals. The season is from November to June.

## Teatro Malibran

Campo del Teatro, 5870
Cannaregio (*vaporetti* 1, 2 and 34, Rialto-B2)
Information and reservations
☎ 041 522 49 97.

Built in 1677, this theatre is a stone's throw from the Grand Canal on the presumed site of Marco Polo's house. It was recently restored and is dedicated to Maria Malibran (1808–1836), a singer with an amazing vocal range, who died tragically young after falling from a horse. Until 2001, some concerts and operas planned for La Fenice will instead take place in its fine auditorium.

## Teatro Fondamente Nuove

Fondamente Nuove,
Cannaregio, 5013
(*vaporetti* 12, 13 and 52,
Fondamente Nuove-C1)
Information and reservations
☎ 041 522 44 98.

A theatre with an interesting programme, which includes world music concerts.

## Teatro a l'Avogaria

Campo S. Sebastiano, 1540
Dorsoduro (*vaporetti* 52 and 82, Zattere-A3)
☎ 041 520 46 50.

This theatre often stages productions in the Venetian language. If your Italian is good, you may recognise the local accent, with its slight lisp, neglect of double consonants and tendency to drop final vowels.

# CINEMAS

## Accademia

Dorsoduro, 1019 (*vaporetti* 1 and 82, Accademia-A2)
☎ 041 528 77 06.

An art cinema showing interesting retrospectives made by Italian and foreign film directors in the original versions.

## CINEMA ADRESSES

### Giorgione

Cannaregio 4612
(*vaporetto* 1, Ca'd'Oro-B1)
☎ 041 522 62 18.

This recently opened cinema, a stone's throw from the Strada Nova, is the only one in the city centre with two screens. It shows mainly experimental films.

### Rossini

S. Marco, 3988 (*vaporetti* 1 and 82, S. Marco-B2)
☎ 041 523 03 22.

The latest films and box office hits. You'll be able to hear Sean Connery and Clint Eastwood speaking Italian behind Piazza San Marco.

### Ritz

S. Marco, 617 (*vaporetti* 1, 14, 52 and 82, S. Zaccaria-B2)
☎ 041 520 44 29.

Like the previous cinema, the Ritz shows mainstream films in Italian, except in a few cases. It's in the Mercerie.

### Videoteca Pasinetti

Palazzo Carminati, Scuola Morosini, San Stae, S. Polo
(*vaporetto* 1, S. Stae-B2)
☎ 041 524 13 20.

The Venice video cinema, where you can see fascinating films in their original language. There are two shows a day, generally at 4pm and 9pm.

### Astra

Via Corfu, 9 (off map)
☎ 041 526 02 89.

### Palazzo del Cinema

Lungomare Marconi
(*vaporetti* 1, 6, 14 and 52, Lido-off map)
☎ 041 27 26 511.

## OPEN-AIR FILM SHOWS

In summer in Campo S. Polo (*vaporetti* 1 and 82, S. Tomà), you can see open-air film shows every evening. During the Mostra, the films taking part in the competition are shown the day after the official performance for those who were unable to be present. The programmes appear in the dailies *Il Gazzettino* and *Nuova Venezia*, as well as in the monthly *Un Ospite di Venezia*.

## CAFÉS AND DISCOS

### Sestiere of San Marco

### Le Bistrot de Venise

Calle dei Fabbri, 4685
S. Marco (*vaporetti* 1 and 82, S. Marco and Rialto-B2)
☎ 041 523 66 51
Every day 9.30-1am.

A bistrot where you can dine late to the sound of music and see cabaret shows.

## THE MOSTRA DEL CINEMA

A film festival to rival that of Cannes takes place in the Lido over the course of a fortnight from late August to early September. The films are shown in the large auditoria of the Palazzo del Cinema and Astra cinema. Don't go thinking you'll be able to get seats for the awards ceremony or a preview – it's quite impossible unless you're lucky enough to be in the cinema business. If you're in Venice during the Mostra, make for the Lido anyway (*vaporetti* 1, 6, 14 and 52 from S. Zaccaria) and take up position on one of the strategically placed

terraces of the Lungomare Marconi. From there, you'll be able to eye the new Sophia Lorens and Marcello Mastroiannis strolling along the seafront at your leisure – to the accompaniment of ear-shattering mopeds and music blasting from convertibles.

### Devil's Forrest

Calle degli Stagneri, 5185
(*vaporetti* 1 and 82, Rialto-B2)
☎ 041 520 06 23
Every day 10am-midnight.

A nice, friendly pub a few minutes from the Rialto, offering a good choice of draught beers and sandwiches if you're feeling

peckish at the end of the evening. You can play darts and backgammon here.

### Haig's
(see restaurants p. 77).

### Harry's Bar
(see restaurants p. 76).

### Vino Vino
Calle del Cafetier, 2007/A
(*vaporetto* 1,
S. M. del Giglio-B2/3)
☎ 041 523 70 27
Every day except Tue.
10.30am-11.30pm.

A quiet, fairly select wine bar where the musicians of La Fenice meet up. The prices are a little steep, but it's a very nice place to visit.

### Al Volto
Calle Cavalli, 4081
(*vaporetti* 1 and 82, Rialto-B2)
☎ 041 522 89 45
Every day except Sun.
10am-2.30pm, 5-10pm.

A warm, very friendly wine bar filled with bottles from floor to ceiling. There are lots of kinds of beer and very good wines to drink with *cichèti*. You have to elbow your way to the bar (there's nowhere to sit). The faithful student clientele is

sometimes joined by gondoliers and watertaxi drivers.

## Sestiere of Dorsoduro

### Linea d'Ombra
(see p. 51).

## Sestiere of Castello

### L'Olandese volante
Campo S. Lio, 5658
(*vaporetti* 1 and 82, Rialto-B2)
☎ 041 528 93 49
Every day except Sun.
10am-midnight (1am Sat.).

A pleasant pub with a good location in Campo S. Lio. Wide choice of beers and sandwiches.

## Sestiere of San Polo

### Caffè dei Frari
Fondamenta dei Frari, 2564
(*vaporetti* 1 and 82, S. Tomà-A2). ☎ 041 524 18 77
Every day except Sun.7.30am-9pm, Sat. 8.30am-9pm.

A nice wood-panelled café on two floors with a mezzanine, right next to the grandiose church of the Frari. Lots of young people and a pleasant atmosphere.

## Sestiere of Santa Croce

### Ai Postali
Fondamenta rio Marin, 821
(*vaporetti* 1, 52 and 82,
Riva di Biasio and Ferrovia-A2)

☎ 041 71 51 56
Every day except Tue.
10am-2pm, 6pm-2am.

A lively young bar with a few tables off the beaten tourist track beside Rio Marin. Good choice of wines and tasty *bruschetta* (garlic bread).

## Sestiere of Cannaregio

### Al Paradiso perduto

(see concerts and operas p. 118).

### The Fiddler's Elbow

Corte dei Pali, 3847 (*vaporetto* 1, Ca' d'Oro-B1)
☎ 041 523 99 30
Every day except Wed. (in winter) 5pm-12.30am.

An Irish pub frequented by a mixture of tourists and young Venetians. Good choice of draught and bottled beers and excellent Irish coffee. Pleasant atmosphere with concerts some evenings.

## The Giudecca

### Harry's Dolci

(see restaurants p. 65).

## DISCOS

### Discobar Acropolis

Lungomare Marconi, 22 Lido (*vaporetti* 1, 6, 14 and 52, Lido-off map)
☎ 041 526 04 66
Every day except Mon., weekends only out of season, 10pm-3am.

The Lido disco-bar overlooks the sea. You can come for an after-dinner drink, to dance, or to be seen during the Mostra del Cinema. A variety of music.

### Martini Scala

Campo S. Fantin, 1983
S. Marco (*vaporetti* 1 and 82, S. M. del Giglio-B2)
☎ 041 522 41 21
Every day except Tue. 10pm-3.30am.

The piano-bar of the Antico Martini restaurant, where you can have a drink in elegant company.

### Club Piccolo Mondo

Calle Contarini, 1056/A Dorsoduro (*vaporetti* 1 and 82, Accademia-A2)
☎ 041 520 03 71
Every day except Tue. 10pm-4am.

A bit old-fashioned, but one of the few discos in the historic centre of Venice. Sixties, seventies and dance music.

## Casanova

**Cannaregio, Lista di Spagna 158/A (*vaporetti* 1, 52 and 82, Ferrovia-A2)**
**☎ 041 275 01 99**
**Every day except Sun., Mon. and Tue. 6pm-4am.**

*The* Venice disco-bar is just a stone's throw from the station, so it's very handy, even if you're staying on the mainland. Its decor is an avant-garde version of the old Venetian palaces. Entry is free and happy hour goes on until 10pm, which is rare in Venice.

### Terra ferma

The liveliest discos are on *terra ferma* (the mainland) in Mestre (frequent trains from S. Lucia station) and the surrounding district. You can either go to Area City (Via Tosatto don Federico, 9 Mestre ☎ 041 95 97 00) or to the Ranch Ca' Noghera (Via Triestina, 222 Tessera (☎ 041 541 53 82, closed Mon.).

## CASINOS

### Palazzo del Casino

**Lungomare Marconi, 4 Lido (*vaporetti* 1, 6, 14, 52 and 82, Lido-off map)**
**☎ 041 529 71 11**
**Every day May-Sep. from 4pm onwards.**

The casino opens in summer in this building on the Lido next to the Palazzo del Cinema and the neo-Moorish Grand Hotel Excelsior. It's a chance to experience all kinds of thrills (roulette, blackjack, slot machines etc.), and to see the luxurious Hôtel des Bains, which was immortalised by Visconti in *Death in Venice*.

### Palazzo Vendramin Calergi

**Calle Larga Vendramin, Cannaregio (*vaporetti* 1 and**
**82, S. Marcuola-B1)**
**☎ 041 529 71 11**
**Every day Oct.-Apr. from 3pm.**

The Venice Casino has its winter quarters on the banks of the Grand Canal, in this superb Renaissance palace dating from the early 16th century, where Richard Wagner died in 1883. It makes a choice setting in which to make a dent in your lire playing roulette, black-jack or other less ruinous games, the slot machines in particular. For a real treat, arrive in a gondola.

# More handy words and phrases

## USEFUL EXPRESSIONS
**I am sorry**
Mi dispiace
**I don't know**
Non lo so
**How?**
Come?
**Pardon me?**
Prego?
**Could you repeat that?**
Può ripetere quello per favore?
**My name is…**
Mi chiamo…
**A lot**
Molto
**Enough**
Abbastanza
**Nothing**
Niente

## AT THE HOTEL
**Hotel**
Albergho
**Bed & breakfast/ guesthouse**
Pensione
**I have a reservation**
Ho una prenotazione
**…for three people**
…per tre persone
**…for three nights**
…per tre notti
**with a double bed**
con un letto matrimoniale
**with twin beds**
con due letti
**Is breakfast included?**
E compresa la prima colazione?
**We are leaving tomorrow morning**
Partiamo domani mattina
**Suitcase**
Valigia

## IN THE RESTAURANT
**I would like…**
Vorrei…

**What is the dish of the day?**
Qual'è il piatto del giorno?
**I would just like something to drink**
Vorrei solo bere qualcosa
**Wine list**
Lista dei vini
**Non smoking**
Non Fumatori
**Baked**
Al forno
**Grilled**
Alla griglia
**Poached**
Cotto in bianco
**Fried**
Fritto
**Steamed**
Al vapore

## MEAT AND FISH
**Meat**
Carne
**Bacon**
Pancetta
**Sausage**
Salsiccia
**Shellfish/seafood**
Molluschi/Frutta di mare
**Cod**
Merluzzo
**Salmon**
Salmone

## VEGETABLES
**Courgettes**
Zucchini
**Aubergines/eggplants**
Melanzane
**French beans**
Fagiolini
**Spinach**
Spinaci
**Mushrooms**
Funghi
**Tomato**
Pomodoro

**Potatoes**
Patate

## SUNDRIES
**Crisps/peanuts**
Patatine/noccioline americane
**Salt/pepper**
Sale/pepe
**Mustard**
Senape
**Sugar**
Zucchero
**Rice**
Riso
**Egg**
Uovo
**Toast**
Pane tostato

## DRINKS
**A glass of…**
Un bicchiere di…
**Tea with milk/lemon**
Thè con latte/limone
**Fruit juice**
Succo di frutta
**Hot chocolate**
Cioccolata
**Sparkling water**
Acqua frizzante

## NUMBERS
| | |
|---|---|
| **1** | Uno |
| **2** | Due |
| **3** | Tre |
| **4** | Quattro |
| **5** | Cinque |
| **6** | Sei |
| **7** | Sette |
| **8** | Otto |
| **9** | Nove |
| **10** | Dieci |
| **11** | Undici |
| **12** | Dodici |
| **13** | Tredici |
| **14** | Quattordici |
| **15** | Quindici |
| **16** | Seidici |

| | |
|---|---|
| **17** Diciasette | |
| **18** Diciotto | |
| **19** Diciannove | |
| **20** Venti | |

## TIME AND DATES
**Morning/afternoon/evening**
La mattina/il pomeriggio/la sera
**Yesterday/today/tomorrow**
Ieri/oggi/domani

### DAYS OF THE WEEK
**Monday**
Lunedì
**Tuesday**
Martedì
**Wednesday**
Mercoledì
**Thursday**
Giovedì
**Friday**
Venerdì
**Saturday**
Sabato
**Sunday**
Domenica

## IN THE TOWN
**Can you tell me the way to…?**
Per andare a…?
**What time does it open?**
A che ora apre?
**What time does it close?**
A che ora chiude?
**Here/there**
Qui/là
**Near/far**
Vicino/lontano
**Opposite**
Di fronte
**Next to**
Accanto a
**On the left/on the right**
A sinistra/a destra
**Straight on**
Sempre dritto
**Entrance/Exit**
Entrata/Uscita
**Change money**

Cambiare
**Bureau de change**
Cambio
**Traveller's cheque**
Assegno turistico
**Cash machine**
Bancomat
**Post box**
Cassetta
**Stamp**
Francobollo
**Telephone**
Telefono

## TRAVELLING
**I want to go to…**
Voglio andare a…
**Do I need to change?**
Devo cambiare?
**Which platform does it leave from?**
Da quale binario parte?
**Bus/coach station**
Stazione di autobus
**Bus stop**
Fermata d'autobus
**Airport**
Aeroporto
**Taxi rank**
Posteggio di taxi
**Car**
Macchina
**Bicycle**
Bicicletta
**On foot**
A piedi
**Passport**
Passaporto
**Timetable**
Orario
**Left luggage**
Deposito bagagli

## SHOPPING
**It's too expensive**
E troppo caro
**Where can I find…?**
Dove posso trovare…?

### SHOPPING FOR CLOTHES AND ACCESSORIES
**Bag**
Borsa

**Belt**
Cintura
**Blouse**
Camicetta
**Bracelet**
Braccialetto
**Coat**
Cappotto
**Dress**
Vestito
**Earring**
Orecchino
**Hat**
Capello
**Leather**
Cuoio
**Jacket**
Giacca
**Jeweller**
Gioielliere, orefice
**Lingerie**
Biancheria intima
**Purse**
Portamonete
**Ring**
Anello
**Scarf**
Sciarpa
**Silk**
Seta
**Socks (or stockings)**
Calze
**Shirt**
Camicia
**Shoes**
Scarpe
**Skirt**
Gonna
**Suit**
Vestito
**Sweater**
Maglietta, golf
**T-shirt**
Maglietta
**Trousers**
Pantaloni
**Tie**
Cravatta
**Tights**
Collant
**Wallet**
Portafoglio

# Conversion tables for clothes shopping

Note that in Italy 'size' has two different translations. For clothes 'la taglia' is size; for shoes, size is 'il numero'.

## Women's sizes

### Shirts/dresses

| U.K | U.S.A | EUROPE |
|-----|-------|--------|
| 8 | 6 | 36 |
| 10 | 8 | 38 |
| 12 | 10 | 40 |
| 14 | 12 | 42 |
| 16 | 14 | 44 |
| 18 | 16 | 46 |

### Sweaters

| U.K | U.S.A | EUROPE |
|-----|-------|--------|
| 8 | 6 | 44 |
| 10 | 8 | 46 |
| 12 | 10 | 48 |
| 14 | 12 | 50 |
| 16 | 14 | 52 |

### Shoes

| U.K | U.S.A | EUROPE |
|-----|-------|--------|
| 3 | 5 | 36 |
| 4 | 6 | 37 |
| 5 | 7 | 38 |
| 6 | 8 | 39 |
| 7 | 9 | 40 |
| 8 | 10 | 41 |

## Men's sizes

### Shirts

| U.K | U.S.A | EUROPE |
|-----|-------|--------|
| 14 | 14 | 36 |
| $14^1/_2$ | $14^1/_2$ | 37 |
| 15 | 15 | 38 |
| $15^1/_2$ | $15^1/_2$ | 39 |
| 16 | 16 | 41 |
| $16^1/_2$ | $16^1/_2$ | 42 |
| 17 | 17 | 43 |
| $17^1/_2$ | $17^1/_2$ | 44 |
| 18 | 18 | 46 |

### Suits

| U.K | U.S.A | EUROPE |
|-----|-------|--------|
| 36 | 36 | 46 |
| 38 | 38 | 48 |
| 40 | 40 | 50 |
| 42 | 42 | 52 |
| 44 | 44 | 54 |
| 46 | 46 | 56 |

### Shoes

| U.K | U.S.A | EUROPE |
|-----|-------|--------|
| 6 | 8 | 39 |
| 7 | 9 | 40 |
| 8 | 10 | 41 |
| 9 | 10.5 | 42 |
| 10 | 11 | 43 |
| 11 | 12 | 44 |
| 12 | 13 | 45 |

### More useful conversions

| 1 centimetre | 0.39 inches | 1 inch | 2.54 centimetres |
|--------------|-------------|--------|------------------|
| 1 metre | 1.09 yards | 1 yard | 0.91 metres |
| 1 kilometre | 0.62 miles | 1 mile | 1. 61 kilometres |
| 1 litre | 1.76 pints | 1 pint | 0.57 litres |
| 1 gram | 0.35 ounces | 1 ounce | 28.35 grams |
| 1 kilogram | 2.2 pounds | 1 pound | 0.45 kilograms |

This guide was written by **Denis Montagnon**
Updated and revised by **Francesca Massarotto** and **Caroline Boissy**,
with the assistance of **Anne-Gaëlle Moutarde**
Translated and edited by **Margaret Rocques**
Series editor **Liz Coghill**
Additional assistance **Claire Wedderburn-Maxwell, Jenny Piening,
Briony Chappell** and **Sofi Mogensen**

We have done our best to ensure the accuracy of the information contained in this guide.
However, addresses, phone numbers, opening times etc. inevitably do change from time
to time, so if you find a discrepancy please do let us know. You can contact us at:
hachetteuk@orionbooks.co.uk or write to us at Hachette UK, address below.

Hachette UK guides provide independent advice. The authors and compilers do not accept any
remuneration for the inclusion of any addresses in these guides.

Please note that we cannot accept any responsibility for any loss, injury or inconvenience
sustained by anyone as a result of any information or advice contained in this guide.

## Photo acknowledgements

*Inside pages*
**Ch. Sarramon**: pp. 10 (c. r.), 11 (c.), 13 (t. l.), 14, 15 (b.), 16 (t.), 17 (c.; t.), 19 (t.), 20 (b. l.), 22 (c. l.), 23 (t. l.), 24 (b. r.; t. r.), 25, 26, 27 (t. l. and r.; b.), 30 (c.), 33 (t. r.), 38 (b.; t. l.), 39 (t. r.; c.; b. r.), 40 (t. l.; b. r.), 42, 43 (t.; c.; b. r.), 44, 45 (c. l; t. c.; b.), 46 (l.), 47 (t. l.; c.), 48 (b.), 49 (c.), 51 (t. r.; b. l.), 52, 53 (t.; c. l. and r.; b.), 55 (t. l.; c. l.; t. c.; b.), 56 (r.), 57 (t. l. and r.), 58, 59 (t. l. and r.), 61 (t. l. and r.), 62 (l.), 63 (c.), 66, 67, 68, 90 (b.r.), 91 (t.), 92 (c.l.), 93 (c.r.), 96 (c.), 97 (t.r.; sweets t.c.); b.l.; b.c.), 99 (c.l.), 100 (b.l.), 102 (c.c.), 104 (b.r.), 105 (b.l.; b.r.), 106 (b.r.), 109 (t.l.; c.c.; b.l.), 112 (b.).
**R. Leslie**: pp. 3, 10 (b.; t.), 12, 13 (b. l.; c.; t. r.), 15 (t.), 16 (b.), 17 (b.), 18 (c.l.; t.), 19 (c.l.; b.), 20 (t.; b. r.), 21 (b. l. and r.), 24 (c.), 27 (c.), 28, 29, 30 (t.r.), 31 (t.; c.), 32 (b.l.; b.r.), 33 (t.; b.), 38 (t. r.), 39 (t. l.), 40 (t. r.), 41, 43 (b. l.), 45 (t. l. and r.), 46 (r.), 47 (t. r.; b.), 49 (t.l.), 50, 54, 55 (t. r.), 56 (l.), 59 (b.), 60, 61 (t. c.; c.), 62 (r.), 63 (t.; b.), 64, 65, 68, 69, 73, 75, 78, 80 (l.), 81 (b.), 82, 83, 88 (c.r.; b.r.), 89, 90 (t.), 92 (t.; b.), 93 (t.; c.l.), 94 (b.l.), 95 (t.r.; c.l.; c.c.), 97 (glass t.c.), 98 (t.c.; c.r.), 99 (t.r.), 100 (t.r.; c.c.), 101, 102 (c.r.; b.c.), 103 (t.l.; t.c.), 104 (b.l.), 105 (t.c.; c.r.; b.c.), 106 (c.c.), 107 (t.r., c.l.), 108 (t.), 109 (c.r.), 110 (t.; b.l.), 111 (c.c.), 112 (t.r.; t.l.; c.d.), 113 (c.c.), 114 (t.r.), 118, 119, 120, 121, 123.
**L. Parrault**: pp. 19 (c. r.), 95 (b.), 103 (b.), 107 (b.r.), 115 (b.l.).
**Hachette**: pp. 11 (b. r.; t. r.), 22 (t.), 23 (b.), 113 (b.).
**Taglia & Incolla**: pp. 30 (b.), 31 (b.), 53 (b. r.), 98 (t.r.; b.c.).
**Mondo Novo Maschere**: p. 23 (t. r.). **Michele Cigogna**: p. 57 (t. c.). **Cipriani**: pp. 75, 81 (t.). **Da Ivo Ristorante**: p. 79. **Gonzales**: p. 88 (t.). **Venetia Studium**: p. 90 (c.l.; c.r.), 91 (b.). **Berengo Fine Arts**: p. 96 (b.), 97 (t.l.). **Rosa Salva**: p. 100 (b.r.). **Marforio**: p. 106 (t.). **Chimento**: p. 108 (b.). **Totem Il Canale**: p. 109 (b.). **F. G. B.**: p. 110 (c. r.). **Gilberto Penzo**: p. 111 (b.). **Nalesso**: p. 113 (t. l.). **A. Barutti**: p. 114 (t. c.). **Gianni Basso**: p. 114 (t.). **Nel Giardino del Tempo**: p. 115 (t. l.). **Michele Gregolin**: p. 115 (t. r.).
**Rights reserved**: pp. 11 (t. l.), 21 (t.).

*Cover*: **Image Bank / D. de Lossy**: t.c.; **Image Bank / Bokelberg**: b.c.; **Pix / J.-P. Fruchet**: c.; front. **Ch. Sarramon**: t.l. and t.r.; c.l. and c.r.; b.l and b.r.

*Back cover*: **Ch. Sarramon**: c.l. b.l.; **R. Leslie**: t.r. and t.l. front.

## Illustrations **Pascal Garnier**
Cartography © **Hachette Tourisme**

If you're staying on a little longer and would like to try some new places, the following pages will provide you with a wide choice of hotels, restaurants and cafés, listed by district, with price (in lire), in which to spend your evenings.

Although you can usually just turn up at a restaurant and have a meal (except in the most prestigious establishments), don't forget to book your hotel several days in advance, or even several months ahead during the Carnival period.

Prices given here are a guide only.

Enjoy your stay!

# STAYING ON
# A LITTLE LONGER

**Hotel Bridge**
Castello 4498
☎ 041 520 52 87
📠 041 520 22 97
Double room
around L336,000.
*A quiet, well-situated hotel a stone's throw from Campo Santi Filippo e Giacomo, near Piazza San Marco. Book in advance.*

**Hotel Rio**
Castello
Campo Santi Filippo e
Giacomo 4356
☎ 041 523 48 10
📠 041 520 82 22
Double room
L160,000-250,000.
*This hotel, very close to Piazza San Marco, overlooks a charming 'campiello'. The prices are very reasonable but there are only fifteen rooms.*

**Hotel Riva**
Castello
Ponte dell'Angelo 5310
☎ 041 522 70 34
📠 041 528 55 51
Double room
around L170,000.
*This hotel near San Zaccaria was recently renovated throughout. It offers a warm welcome in addition to the tasteful decor.*

**Hotel Bauer Grunwald**
San Marco
Campo S. Moisé 1459
☎ 041 520 70 22
📠 041 520 75 57
Double room
L410,000-790,000.
*This four-star hotel is in the heart of the city, very near Piazza San Marco and the café Florian. Its marvellous terrace overlooks the Grand Canal.*

**Hotel Saturnia & International**
San Marco
Via XXII marzo 2398
☎ 041 520 83 77
📠 041 520 71 31.
*This four-star hotel is in the smart part of Venice, where you'll find the big names of Italian fashion.*

**Locanda Sturion**
San Polo
Calle Sturion 679
☎ 041 523 62 43
📠 041 522 83 78

Double room
L200,000-310,000.
*This superbly located hotel offers three-star comfort. With a little luck, you'll get a room with a view of the Rialto and Grand Canal.*

**Hotel Falier**
Santa Croce
Salizada S. Pantalon 130
☎ 041 71 08 82
📠 041 520 65 54
Double room
L150,000-280,000.
*This recently renovated two-star hotel is near Piazzale Roma. Parking is available.*

**Hotel Sofitel**
Santa Croce
Piazzale Roma 245
☎ 041 71 04 00
📠 041 71 03 94
Double room
L650,000-720,000.
*As part of the Sofitel chain, this hotel comes with a guarantee of quality. It's in Piazzale Roma, where you can park. At certain times of the year, there are special offers (contact the hotel direct).*

**Hotel Carlton Executive**
Santa Croce 578
☎ 041 71 84 88
📠 041 71 90 61
Double room
L260,000-520,000.
*If you arrive in Venice by train, you'll see this hotel just opposite the station as you come out of the station. It has all the comfort of a four-star hotel.*

**Hotel La Calcina**
Dorsoduro
Zattere 780
☎ 041 520 64 66
📠 041 522 70 45
Double room
L180,000-280,000.
*This charming hotel lies off the beaten tourist track opposite the Canale della Giudecca. It's quiet and well-kept and has a sun terrace on the roof – a rarity not to be missed.*

**Hotel Belle Arti**
Dorsoduro 912
☎ 041 522 62 30
📠 041 528 00 43
Double room

L220,000-340,000.
*All the rooms in this three-star hotel in the Accademia district are furnished in the Venetian style, and are as comfortable as can be. Very good value for money.*

**Hotel Villa Rosa**
Cannaregio
Calle Misericordia 389
☎ 041 71 89 76
📠 041 71 65 69
Double room
L160,000-190,000.
*Near the station, this little hotel with a terrace offers the comfort of a two-star hotel.*

**Hotel Bernardi Semenzato**
Cannaregio
Calle dell'Oca 4366
☎ 041 522 72 57
📠 041 522 24 24
Double room
L100,000-160,000.
*A small, recently renovated establishment tucked away in an alleyway typical of the district. The owner is a mine of information.*

**Hotel Eden**
Cannaregio
Rio Terrà Maddalena 2357
☎ 041 524 40 05
📠 041 72 02 28
Double room
L190,000-280,000.
*This hotel, near the station in the Santa Marcuola district, has been tastefully renovated and overlooks a charming little courtyard.*

# HOTELS

### Caffè Noir
Dorsoduro
Calle Lunga San Pantalon
3805
☎ 041 71 09 25.
*This trendy new café, just a minute from Campo San Margherita, is an Internet café, sandwich bar and 'tea room' rolled into one.*

### Sottosopra
Dorsoduro
Calle San Pantalon 3740
☎ 041 524 21 77.
*You can have a drink and a sandwich here as you listen to the music and maybe even catch a concert.*

### Osteria Vecia Carbonera
Cannaregio
Rio Terà Madalena 2329
☎ 041 71 03 76.
*People come to this café near the station for its music, regional wines and view of the canal. You almost feel as if you could reach out and touch the water from here.*

### Alla Mascareta
Castello
Calle Lunga S. M. Formosa 5183
☎ 041 523 07 44.
*A select restaurant near San Marco, with an excellent choice of wines and temporary exhibitions by local artists.*

### Sacro e Profano
San Polo
Sottoportego dei Orefici 502
☎ 041 520 19 31.
*A typically Venetian bistrot under the arcades of the Ponte di Rialto, where a large number of wines and original 'cicheti' will be offered to you.*

### Osteria all'Arco
San Polo
Calle de l'Ochialer 436
☎ 041 520 56 66.
*Another very good osteria near the Ponte di Rialto. It's the ideal place for a break after going round the market.*

### Vini da Pinto
San Polo
Campo delle Beccarie 367
☎ 041 522 45 99.

*In fine weather, you can have lunch outside opposite the 'pescheria' (Rialto fish market). If you're passing through, stop for a drink and a 'crostino al bacalà' (cod sandwich) made on the premises.*

### Randon
Dorsoduro
Campo San Barnaba
2852
☎ 041 522 44 10.
*A wine bar with an excellent selection of Italian and foreign wines. There is a set meal at lunchtime with a choice of main courses.*

### Pizzeria Novecento
San Polo
Campiello dei Sansoni
900
☎ 041 522 65 65.
*A pizzeria a stone's throw from the Rialto where you can eat good pizzas to the sound of jazz. Live music on Thursdays.*

### La Palazzina
Cannaregio
Ponte delle Guglie 1509
☎ 041 71 77 25.
*This typically Venetian restaurant, not far from the station, naturally offers pizzas. Friendly atmosphere.*

### Osteria Anice Stellato
Cannaregio
Fondamenta de la Sensa
3272
☎ 041 72 07 44.
*This osteria near the Ghetto isn't easy to find, but it's the place to come to sample real Venetian fish cuisine.*

### Pizzeria al Faro
Cannaregio
Ghetto Vecchio 1181
☎ 041 275 07 94.
*A pizzeria in the heart of the old Ghetto that serves special pizzas for hearty appetites. You're assured of a warm welcome here.*

# RESTAURANTS

In case you haven't found what you're looking for in the Shopping section, we've provided a further selection of unusual and original shops below.

## Beba
San Polo
Campo delle Beccarie 370/A
☎ 041 523 08 19.
*Beba (who has a diploma in pictorial decoration) will welcome you with a smile to her tiny workshop opposite the Rialto fish market.*

## Nason Daniele
Castello
Calle Barberia delle Tole 6468
☎ 041 522 81 13.
*This master craftsman makes traditional gilded papier mâché masks while you watch. It's fantastic.*

## Tragicomica
San Polo
Calle dei Botteri 1566
☎ 041 72 11 02.
*Don't miss this shop near the Rialto if you're fond of masks, Carnival costumes and the traditional characters of the Commedia dell'Arte.*

## Costantini Glass Beads
San Marco
Calle Zaguri 2627
☎ 041 521 07 89.
*Near Campo San Maurizio, you'll find flowers, jewellery, little bags and embroidery for your curtains, both modern and antique, made of Murano glass beads.*

## La Gondola
San Marco 1166
☎ 041 520 70 15.
*When you enter this gallery behind Piazza San Marco, you'll find a wide choice of Murano glass chandeliers and sculptures. Don't miss the collections by the great names of glass-making.*

## Artistica Ferro
Santa Croce
Calle Lunga 2137
☎ 041 520 04 90.
*Wrought iron in all its forms is worked here by craftsmen. Any design, whether functional or decorative, can be made for the home, including copies of antique ironwork. You can also have pieces restored here.*

## Laberintho
San Polo 2236
☎ 041 71 00 17.
*A goldsmith's workshop where original jewellery is made to order.*

## Mare de Carta
Santa Croce
Fondamenta dei Tolentini 222
☎ 041 71 63 04.
*This bookshop specialises in works on the world's seas and oceans. There are books in every language, as well as maps, portolans (sailing manuals) and a number of sections on navigation.*

SHOPPING

# A BOAT RIDE ON THE BRENTA CANAL

The 38km/23 1/2mile canal was built on the Brenta in the 16th century and was originally used to transport people and goods. Linking Padua and Venice, it takes in some magnificent villas. In the 18th century, the *Il Burchiello* made its way along the canal, transporting lords, merchants, actors and artists. The boat is still in service today, and this mini-cruise, lasting around 10 hours, holds many treasures. It stops on the way to allow passengers to visit two villas in particular which are open to the public, the Villa Pisani and the Villa Serinam Wildamnn Foscari. These former residences of Venetian aristocrats were once the scene of balls, firework displays and concerts. The copses were used to conceal orchestras playing the airs of Vilvaldi and Pergolese. Many other villas border the canal, but they aren't all open to visitors, and unfortunately are very often no longer maintained. The boat runs on Tuesdays, Thursdays and Saturdays from early April to late October. The Ponte di Giardinetti next to Piazza San Marco is the departure point for the trip in Venice (leaving at 8.45am and arriving in Padua at 7pm). The ticket price includes entry to the villas but not the 45-minute return journey by coach or train.

# BOAT RIDE

# NOTES

# NOTES

81·00
wed - Sat
209.   Santa Marcina.